The Other Side of My Life

A personal journey into my unknown past, in search of the "other side" of my life.

D. Gary Deatherage

Winston-Derek Publishers, Inc.
Pennywell Drive—P.O. Box 90883
Nashville, TN 37209

PUBLISHED BY WINSTON-DEREK PUBLISHERS, INC.
Nashville, Tennessee 37205

Library of Congress Catalog Card No: 89-51423
ISBN: 1-55523-275-2

Printed in the United States of America

This book is dedicated to Dad and Mom, who nurtured me with all their love; to my darling wife and friend, Susan, whose understanding, support, advice, and endless hours of typing helped make this project possible; to all those from The Other Side who are now part of my life; and to Aunt Betty and Christina for their unselfish guidance along the way.

Prologue

It was January 1, 1943, about one o'clock in the afternoon, when I scampered across the reception room at the Children's Home to two people I'd never seen before. My nurse, Miss Kiss, watched me carefully. She had been caring for me since my arrival from the hospital where I had recently undergone surgery. I had been suited up in a sailor outfit and prepared for this visit—the most important meeting of my young life. Miss Kiss was right. This man and woman looked to be kind and loving. I ran straight to my new dad, and he was delighted. My new mom was carefully looking me over. She knew I had some Italian blood and was wondering how dark I would be. When she saw my blue eyes and felt the warmth the three of us were sharing, acceptance was swift. Thank God! Even though I was only eighteen months old, somehow I knew this was my chance, at last, for a home with love. There was an unexplainable urgency in my hurry to meet these unfamiliar people. Indeed, I was propelled to them as though I had just escaped from the very gates of Hell.

Mom and Dad had indelibly etched in my mind the poignant scene of our union at the Children's Home . . . it was the curtain raiser to my new life. The drama of that first day was often recited to me during my childhood. While my life was beginning anew, the curtain on another stage was falling. The cast of characters were fading into oblivion as the footlights dimmed. The last act of my other life had ended . . . there were no encores or rave reviews. The script to that tragic and amazing story was lost . . .

until now.

The exact year, I'm not sure. It was a long time ago. I was maybe nine or ten years old when my Mom and Dad sat down with me and told me I was a very special person. I was adopted! They wanted me to know how much they loved me, as much as if I had been their natural child. They told me I was eighteen months old when I came to them and that they had waited many years for me to come along. They remembered how I had run across the room to them at the Children's Home, and that we had chosen each other, whereas other families had to accept what came. Above all else, they assured me no matter what life brings we belonged to each other.

GARY

The Box

Twenty-four years after that New Year's Day my dad gave me a gift. In January 1967, eighteen months after Mom passed away, Dad presented me with a stationery box stuffed with letters about me and my adoption. He didn't say much, and I wasn't sure he wanted me to have it. He had recently remarried, and I think this was part of letting go of the past, as well as the result of house cleaning to make room for his new wife's belongings. I had never seen or known of this cache of papers. My parents had always seemed to be very open with me, and for these documents to exist without my knowledge made me wonder how straight-forward they had really been.

Dad had brought his bride of two months to Fort Worth to meet my wife, Susan and me. He slipped me the box just as they were leaving for California. Easing his arm around me, he said, "Gary, I think you should have this. They're medical and adoption records about your past. They're yours to keep and do with as you wish." By the thick quality of his voice I could tell it was an emotional moment for him. We embraced and he left quickly, as though he didn't want to discuss it further.

I really didn't realize the significance or the power of the box's contents. I had matter-of-factly taken it from Dad, and forgotten about it until a few days later. It was a dreary day outside and there was nothing better to do, so I sat down in the middle of our bed and proceeded to examine the gift Dad had reluctantly passed on to me. It was about the size of a child's shoe box, ivory colored with dark brown ends, and an embossed cameo on top. It was secured by a flap that snapped shut. My mom had written in blue pen at the top of the box "Gary Baby Records," which had faded over the years. I opened the top and saw the box was crammed full of old letters. The musty smell told me this box had not been disturbed for many years. At the same time, there was a perfumed and moth ball scent that was an unmistakable clue that it had been stored deep within my mother's clothes closet. Secrets from the past were buried here; this was a time capsule full of information to be consumed.

Home

We lived in Oxnard, a small town in Southern California. My dad was a banker and my mom a school teacher. As in any small town everybody knew everybody. My mother taught first grade and had all the children of the city's fathers in her class at one time or another. She was my first-grade teacher, too. My dad was at the same bank for many years. When I came to live with them they were both in their early forties and were pretty much set in their ways. I came to an established home.

The three of us fit comfortably in our home on "G" Street. When I turn the pages of my mind's diary back to the earliest times, things are recorded there that I haven't thought of in forty years. Mom's dark wooded upright piano, with a metronome perched on top, filled a corner of our dining room, where I spent many hours practicing. In the kitchen we had a refrigerator with a funny looking coil apparatus on top. This was at a time when the iceman made deliveries to those residences with iceboxes, and my friends and I would follow the truck up and down our street hoping to get a chunk. Our breakfast room had big windows which swung open allowing my Mom to "yoo-hoo" at our next door neighbor for a moment or two of gossip which was usually more like an hour or two. Our "automatic" washing machine was equipped with a wringer and when Mom wasn't looking, I'd shove various items through it for effect. I remember lying on the living room rug in front of our radio listening to the "Whistler" or the "Jack Benny Hour."

Since Mom and Dad worked, we had a maid who came several times a week. A man came once a week to look after the lawn and garden. I remember them well.

The maid was black and she was a very happy person. She looked very much like "Aunt Jemima." While she worked, she was always humming a tune. I liked her a lot. She made lots of cookies and told me stories.

The gardener was Portuguese. He didn't speak English very well. He had a wild look about him that made me always a little bit afraid of him.

Our backyard had a well-stocked goldfish pond, many fruit trees and gardens. A large land turtle roamed freely about and was often the object of our dog's curiosity. There was a guest house out back where Grandpa stayed while he lived with us. We had a lathhouse that was always cool and mossy and full of exotic ferns and plants. Behind our property was nothing but open farm fields and the city airport was two miles away.

Forty years ago the population of Oxnard was about eighteen–thousand. The city, on a flat fertile plain near the California coast, was an agricultural community. There was a downtown business district, and two residential areas. Railroad tracks separated the disadvantaged and migrant farm laborers from the rest of the town, and was simply referred to as "across the tracks." We rarely went there, except when our maid needed transportation. Central to our town was a beautiful Catholic Church, constructed with red brick and trimmed in white. Its' spires touched the sky. Many of the streets were lined with trees, each street with a different variety. Homes in our neighborhood were highlighted with colorful gardens and well-manicured lawns. Tall palm trees lined one of the streets which led down-town to a small park. There was a pagoda situated in the center of the park with four massive evergreen trees surrounding it. At Christmas time the trees were lighted and musicians played carols near the pagoda.

My memories go beyond sight. I can still hear the distant train whistle that cut through the night air as I lay in bed waiting for sleep to come. We had a sugarbeet factory, which not only produced sugar, but gave a wonderful unique aroma when the beets were being processed. It was close to a brown sugar smell. That aroma permeated the air throughout our town. The factory had a baritone whistle that marked the beginning and end of shifts. It was the pulse of our town. Fog occasionally rolled in from the nearby coast, creating a cool dampness that was invigorating. What fond memories.

I will always remember the perfect chemistry of my parents' interrelationship, their oneness of purpose and devotion to each other. Mom was the one to get things moving, while Dad provided the stability and direction. She was the open communicator, while he was reserved and contemplative.

My mom was born and raised in Southern California. Her family was of German Protestant background. She had two younger brothers. They were a very close-knit family. Mom was about 5' 6", medium build, with a fair complexion, light brown hair and blue eyes. She loved children and dedicated her life to teaching. The font in my church where my youngest son was baptized, is dedicated to her memory.

I remember one night in January, 1949, when she got me up about two o'clock in the morning, to see it snowing outside. Living near the coast, snow was a rare occurrence—about once every hundred years or so. Mom cheerfully knocked on the door of every neighborhood house where there were kids, and got them up. The chance that the snow would last till morning was slim. There were snowmen, snowball fights and the sound of children laughing throughout the night.

As it turned out, the snow remained the next day, and we had a school holiday. It was probably the first snow holiday in our city's history.

My dad was born and raised in Kansas City. He had a younger sister. She was my favorite aunt. She was the sweetest person. My dad's heritage was English Protestant. He was 5'8", medium build, light completion, with dark brown hair and eyes. His mother died when he was nine years old. Various aunts helped my grandpa raise him and his sister.

When Dad was very young—maybe eight—he developed a boyhood friendship that would last a lifetime. His friend's name was William Dillenbeck, also of Kansas City. They were like brothers. With the loss of his mother, Dad spent much of his time at the Dillenbecks, and they treated him like one of the family. Dad came out to California in 1927. Bill followed several years later.

Bill was an important part of my life. I fondly called him "Unc," but officially, he was my Godfather. He was an English Professor and taught at several private schools, the last being Harvard School in North Hollywood.

Letters

I sorted the letters into two stacks. The first group dealt with my early medical history. The year I came home with my parents there were no less than six letters relating to my health. My parents and pediatrician were concerned about my low resistance to sickness and generally weak physical state. Efforts were put in motion to build my strength. With all my physical problems, I wonder if my folks had second thoughts about the quality of merchandise they received.

A large part of my physical problem seemed to hinge around a hernia operation I'd had in November 1942, just before my adoption. Other medical documents dealt with various health situations over a ten year period. My mother kept everything. I couldn't have known it when I first read those letters, but the hernia operation would be a critical

7

piece to my life's puzzle twenty years later.

Soon I had little piles of letters all over our bed. I had separated the medical papers by years and content, segregating the health statistic records and the letters from my doctor. The other letters were from the Children's Home Society of California, which I had placed in chronological order. The first letter from the Children's Home Society was dated February 27, 1941. It acknowledged receipt of my parent's application for a child, which they had sent a week earlier. The letter read:

Dear Friends:

Your application for a child has been duly received. You may be sure it will be given every consideration. You know, however, that it is necessary for us, in all cases, to write to the four references given, and then wait for their replies. At the end of a month or two, if we have heard nothing, we write to the applicant for a new reference or references.

After this has been done, one of our field workers will visit your home and talk with you. As our field workers have to go to homes all over the state, you can well understand that it may be several months before she can reach you. Moreover, it is necessary for our visitors to write and verify marriages and divorces, if any. Usually this means writing to a distant state. Sometimes the county clerks wait for two or three months (from nine to twelve) before we can send you notice that your name has been approved.

I am writing all this because after a couple has made a written application for a child, they feel they just can't wait. There is really nothing we can do to hurry things along.

Don't let the delay tempt you to try to get a child by yourself. Such selection requires skilled and experienced people to study the child's background and inheritance. You want the kind of child as near as possible like one which would have been born to you.

That's the kind we hope to select for you.

Most Sincerely Yours,
Children's Home Society of California

What patience my parents must have had. I can imagine how frustrating it must have been, adding up all those months as though time was static. The slow bureaucratic process was a necessary evil. My folks could do nothing but continue with resolve. Consider, up to a year just for the privilege of being approved, and then God only knew how long before the "right" child would come along.

The Children's Home sent a field representative to visit my folks a month later. On the back of that first letter my mom had written out sixty boy's and girl's names, obviously preparing for the day of good news.

I read the last paragraph of the first letter from the Children's Home Society several times. So, I was the result of their skilled and experienced "born to you" matching abilities? My background and inheritance seemed so different from my folks. I never looked like I was born to my mom and dad, much to my consternation. My Italian inheritance shaded my skin and spiced my disposition. In the winter time when my mom or dad introduced me to someone there would be the inevitable comment, "My, what a nice tan you have for this time of year." What could I say? I knew exactly what they were thinking as the comparative stares bounced back and forth between me and my folks. I don't ever remember hearing anyone comment that there was the slightest resemblance. I would have loved to hear that.

There were times when we'd have arguments, and I could feel my blood boil. When I lost my temper I realized how ugly I was compared to their quiet control, and I felt badly. Sometimes I'd mentally create what their natural child would have looked and acted like so I could somehow measure up. At the same time, Mom and Dad realized my individuality and made accommodations for it. Ours was a strong, healthy heterogeneous family.

9

Apparently there was no communication between the Children's Home Society (CHS) and my folks until August of the following year. In the box was a penciled draft of a letter my folks sent to the CHS. It read as follows:

August 3, 1942

Dear Miss Staunton,
On February 22, 1941 we made application for a child. A few weeks later Miss Galligher visited our home and we received a letter of CHS approval. Since that time we have received no other response. We have hesitated to write before as the letter requested prospective parents to be patient.
From August 1941 until June 1942 we have had our five year old nephew with us, due to an accident in which his mother was injured. However, she has fully recovered and he has returned home leaving our home quite empty. Please let us hear from you.

Sincerely,

The next letter was from the CHS, which came a week later. It was short and to the point. The meat of the letter simply said, "It was nice to have a letter from you and we are sorry we can't say to you, "Yes, we have a baby for you." This disappointing news came eighteen months after first hearing from the Children's Home Society.

During this time, (as mentioned in Mom's letter), my cousin came to live with them for ten months. My parents had jumped at the chance to have him stay with them. It's a pity he hadn't developed his ability to construct tree forts yet, as we had a large tree out back just waiting to be settled. Out of three aunts and uncles, he was the only first cousin, and was the closest I came to having a brother. We had great fun together, even though he was several years older than I.

I remember the fabulous tree forts he built. The last one was high in a tree situated in a small canyon behind his Santa Barbara home. It had three floors. The only thing it didn't have was plumbing.

One time we were attacked by three kids and had a terrific dirt clod fight. Since one floor was devoted to ammo and refreshment provisions, the enemy didn't have a chance.

The same cousin was always pulling some kind of practical joke on me. He must have had stock in a local magic shop as I was his favorite victim for hand buzzers, shockers, trick handcuffs and other diabolical items. His family usually came for Thanksgiving and Christmas. That's when I got caught up on all the latest gags.

Finally the letter my folks had been waiting for came. It was dated December 22, 1942. The letter read in part:

I have been thinking about you as I read over your application. Just now we have a little boy who I am anxious to place in the right home. I have known about him since he was born on June 3, 1941. He is an attractive child with dark eyes, dark hair, and a fair complexion. He has some Italian blood.

His mother is English descent and quite blonde, and I know her and her background rather well. I know his father and much about his people. I also know the child's half-brother and sister. They are delightful children. He has possibilities. He has personality. I believe he would be happy in your home and I think you might be interested in him.

I would consider him a handsome child, and I wonder if you would be interested in seeing him. May I hear from you.

Sincerely yours,

What a fascinating letter! On the first reading when I got to the second sentence of the first paragraph where it said,

"We have a little boy," my heartbeat picked up and adrenaline was moving. I looked up and quickly glanced around the room to be sure of no interruptions. I read the letter maybe ten times while planted in the middle of our bed, surrounded by personal treasures from the box.

The immediate thing that struck me was the embodiment of time in the letter. First, my parent's application was over two years old, and now there was an urgency in the midst of the holidays to come see a child. Second, the social worker had known about me since I was born eighteen months earlier, but "just now," she was anxious to place me in the right home. What in hell was going on? Was there something wrong?

Almost two decades later a social worker at the Children's Home would confide that indeed something was wrong. As she scanned my file the wretched truth of my life was revealed. She didn't want to tell me, but I insisted. The records chronicled acts of abuse and torment during the last months before I came to the Home. Apparently, a phantom from my past had stalked me and had turned my life into a living nightmare.

And the letter said I had a half brother and sister. What a surprise that was! Other than being "delightful," I wondered what they were like. I sat there trying to picture them as I had always wanted brothers and sisters. Did they look like me? Did I act like them? How much older were they than I? The mind is a marvelous instrument, and as I fed it bits and pieces of information, a composite picture took shape. The figures of a boy and girl came alive, but were ghost-like. They were playing hopscotch in front of an apartment house. They were dark like me, and I could tell they were my brother and sister. Somehow they knew I was watching them play and they were taunting me. Was this a daydream or some kind of ESP encounter? It was a haunting experience which I played over and over again.

I'm sure my parents had their share of anxieties. Mom had written in pencil on the back of the letter:

1) How much Italian blood? 2) Are parents living? 3) Are brothers and sisters living? 4) What past illnesses? 5) House broke? I liked that last one—I hoped I was! My mom was beside herself with joy and hope. She had drafted a little note to the Home Society.

It read in part:

> *Such a surprise we received from you on Thursday! we had hoped to be able to come down and see and talk with you in regard to the little boy. Have tried to reach you by phone several times! But of course realize you must have a holiday, too.*

The day after Christmas Mom and Dad finally got hold of Mrs. Staunton and arranged to come see me on new Year's Day, 1943, at the Children's Home, about one o'clock. Miss Kiss, one of the resident nurses, presented me to my mom and dad. The sailor suit I wore that day had been saved for me. Dad has proudly told me over the years how I first ran to him and then to Mom. I was such a good deal that they took me home with them.

My arrival was cause for much excitement and happiness to my new parents. My grandfather lived with them at the time and captured the moment in his letter dated January 4, 1943.

> *Now for the big news. Floyd and Helen got word just before Christmas that a boy was awaiting them down at the Home, so on New Year's day they went to L.A. and picked him up. A fine boy 18 months old, with a pretty smile and good disposition. When I got home that eve, Helen had him in the kitchen with her, so had him march out to meet me. He took to me right away, and to all the family. He certainly is a darling. They had their application in for three years, and this was their first call. Until they can get a maid, one of Helen's married friends will look after him*

13

while she is in school. It certainly has made a change in the household. Floyd busy washing out the undies, hung them on the line in the back porch and I ran into them in the dark, going out. Well things have changed in our household.

Grampa was a kind, gentle and loving person, and fun to be with. At the same time he had a formal, quiet manner about him. Even though he was retired, he often wore a three-piece suit when he went for a walk or to dinner. Our evening meal was punctual, and rather formal. I was expected to mind my manners. Dad, Grampa and I took turns saying the meal blessing. Once Grampa sedately bowed his head and said, "Good bread, good meat, good God let's eat!" There were smiles around the table, except Mom who was not happy with Grampa for saying that prayer in my presence. There were several other mealtime incidents that added spice to our lives. Grampa died in his sleep when I was nine, and Dad took him back to Kansas City for burial. It was a sad time for us.

Shortly after my placement a letter came from the Children's Home Society giving my birth and health statistics. It read in part:

Gary was operated on for Hernia in November 1942. He made splendid recovery. His Wasserman was taken, result negative. His birth facts show he was born June 3, 1941. Full term baby. Weighed 7 lbs. at birth. Spontaneous delivery. Six hour labor.

May I congratulate you and your husband. He should be a fine fellow. His disposition will improve with adjustment and good health.

In the time we knew Gary, he needed help in building up his physical strength. Tonsils and adenoids may need attention later.

I am enclosing Gary's ration book. I hope to see you sometime this month. I'll gather all details possible from our file, and thus help you to understand the situation as fully as possible.

The reference to my ration book reminded me that all this was happening right in the middle of World War II. Dad had a physical problem that kept him out of the service. When I read the part about gathering details to "help you understand the situation as fully as possible", I wondered how much dad and Mom really knew.

Were they aware that both the blood of a powerful underworld figure and the criminally insane flowed through the veins of their new son? Had the lady at the Children's Home told Mom and Dad of my first adopted family? I suspect these particulars were unknown to my parents as they have been to me, until recently.

After a year of home visits and close scrutiny, the Children's Home Society of California gave final consent for the official legal adoption. Not long after that my parents received a letter from a law firm which read in part:

Re: Adoption of Marcus Gary Kullberg. You will find enclosed herewith form of petition for adoption of the above named child under the name of David Gary Deatherage.

So my name was Marcus Gary Kullberg—in my previous life. My parents called me Gary since that's what I had been called when they came for me. If my first name was Marcus, why did my family from the "other side" call me Gary? Was the name Marcus from my Italian heritage? So many questions came from all these revelations. There was one other curious thing. My mother had written the names Andrew and Rebecca Kullberg on the back of an envelope in the box. Were these names of my brother and sister, or mother and father? Where she obtained those names I'll probably never know, but they were the only keys, if I ever really wanted to unlock my past.

I decided they had to be my natural mother's and her husband's names. They didn't seem to be Italian, and the chance was good that I'd have my natural mother's last name. But how did Mom get them? The Children's Home people wouldn't have divulged such information.

Mom wrote a short thank you note to the Children's Home Society, which read in part:

Just a little note to say "Thank You" for the help and kindness to our family during our adoptive period. You certainly were helpful and we always enjoyed your visits so much.

Our young son Gary is getting to be quite a young man now. He talks quite a bit now and he is such a good natured little fellow—always smiling. He has been able to get out and play with some of the children in the neighborhood since the weather has been better and he surely has the time of his life.

Please do come by and see us. I should like to send in some dresses for a little girl when we see you. And don't forget if you are looking for a place to lay your head we will enjoy having you stay with us.

Hoping to see you soon.

Mom's comment about my being "good natured" reminded me that everyone remarked what a happy child I was. The folks said I woke up in the morning with a smile on my face. How times have changed! I doubt Sue and the boys would accuse me of anything but loud snores now. As a boy, childhood friends nicknamed me Smiley, which stuck with me through high school.

When I had finished reading the last piece I could find in the box, almost three hours had flown by that afternoon in late January 1967. I unwound from my Buddha-like position on the bed and walked around. I hadn't moved a muscle during the hypnotic-like consumption of my past. I was in a daze. When the reality of it hit, I was ecstatic with my discovery, much like an archaeologist would be with a new find. I called Susan in to share what the box had given up.

Susan quietly listened as I guided her through the various stacks of letters on our bed. The part that intrigued her most was the names; Marcus Gary, Andrew and Rebecca Kullberg. She asked what I planned to do with this intoxicating information, and I replied that someday I might try to find my natural parents. She looked at me quizzically and asked, "Why?" I'm not sure I gave much of an answer then, other than to say that an unexplainable inner force was driving me. "An unexplainable inner force?" she retorted. She didn't seem impressed with the answer and let me know it with her sarcastic stare.

I became defensive and asked, "How could you possibly understand my feelings? You've always known your genetic heritage." Sue could tell I was becoming irritated at that point and let it drop. She and I both knew my odyssey was just beginning. It had the potential of turning all our lives upside down.

There were twenty-six letters in all. At the bottom of the box I found some other odds an ends: My first birthday party invitation from "my friend Charlie", my first valentines, my first cards to my dad and mom, and some old photos. It was a treasure of information about myself. I read those letters so often I could almost recite them from memory.

The stage was set. It was like beginning a good mystery novel. The secrets of my past were starting to unravel.

Boyhood

It's interesting to me how my parents were able to adjust and incorporate me into their conservative lives. I'm not sure I could have done it. After years of orderly adult living—to have a kid almost at the terrible twos stage drop into their routine—was incredible. While in their forties, no less, that's insanity. Or love.

Tradition was important in our family. Religious holidays and birthdays received much attention, and the anticipation of their coming was great. Christmas was my favorite time of year. Our home was always full of people and the titillating smells and sounds of Christmas. The same relatives and friends came year after year.

Kids look forward to Christmas for the presents, sweets and good cheer. I was no different. We went to the midnight Episcopal Mass on Christmas Eve and opened our presents on Christmas morning. My favorite Christmas gift as a youngster was an electric train. I was ten or eleven. It was a fabulous set. Dad and I had it sprawled all over the living room and part of the dining room floors. He loved it as much as I, and we played with it for hours.

I was fascinated by real trains as well. So was Dad. He and I would go down to the train station and watch trains go in and out by the hour. One time as we were watching a big steam engine move back and forth, toting railroad cars here and there, the engineer motioned for Dad and me to come over. He invited us to get in the big steam engine cab with him! We had been there so many times he felt like he knew us. I became scared and begged Dad not to go. The engine was gigantic, loud and made the ground shake. It was OK from a distance, but getting in the belly was something else again. Dad tried to talk me into it, but I adamantly declined. I think he was disappointed, but understood.

My uncommon enchantment with "choo-choo" trains was deep-rooted. During the first six months of life I was a frequent train traveler. Mommy Dear often included my sister and me when she journeyed to New York. Our accommodations for the Los Angeles to New York trip were first class, including a pullman stateroom and separate roomette for the nurse who cared for me. When I came along, my mother took precautions against being met by newspaper reporters, or mobbed by fans.

My birthdays were real productions up until I was thirteen or so. About twenty of my friends were invited. That meant close to twenty mothers came also. Since my birthday was in June, party headquarters was our backyard. Mom and Dad made them gala events. Not long ago I was sifting through old photos of my fifth through seventh birthdays. I was certainly the center of attention, and smiling from ear to ear. But I swear, of the twenty or so children that were there, I only recognized five or six. I didn't know I had so many friends.

In the early years my life was full and active, yet simple and slow-paced. Mom kept close tabs on me. It appeared that other children had more freedom than I, and my friends would let me know it. Naps and playing time were highly regulated, seemingly to my disadvantage, which of course wasn't the case. Mom was particularly cautious about my security. From the outset, she instilled the habit and idea that I must always keep her informed of my whereabouts, and if she caught me off schedule, I heard about it. Also, I was never, under any circumstances, to accept a ride or anything from strangers. The seed of distrust was planted deep within and cultivated often.

Before I was old enough for kindergarten, I stayed with a lady who lived across the street from the elementary school where Mom taught. I could see the windows of her classroom and I'm sure she could see me when I was playing in the yard. My close proximity was necessary for Mom.

I can still remember the high-ceilinged bedroom and window shades that flapped in the afternoon breeze where I took my nap. There was a little girl named Carolyn who lived four houses down the block and was a frequent playmate. We would play "cars" by the hour. She was a good friend for many years. In fact, at the wise old age of twelve we went to a Halloween party together and she was the first young lady I had ever kissed with passionate feelings. That was when I realized why girls were different from boys, and it was good.

When I was three and a half years old an incident occurred in Los Angeles, that had my parents known the bizarre and mysterious connection, it would have caused them grave concern. On December 29, 1944, a woman forcibly entered a Los Angeles residence and was apprehended by the FBI for attempted kidnapping. The January 17, 1945 edition of the *Los Angeles Times* broke the story with front-page headlines and a quarter-page, full-length photo of the suspect. The woman had mistakenly thought the child she was pursuing to be at the Brentwood house address, when actually he was far removed from the Los Angeles area. The child she had hoped to kidnap was me.

As a boy, there were the usual fights, name calling, hand gestures and nose picking. I went through the typical boyhood phase of playing doctor and house with the neighborhood girls. When I ran across the birthday invitation from "my friend Charlie", preserved in the box, it brought to mind an event I'm not particularly proud of—the "dog shit" episode.

Charlie and I were nine at the time and had been searching for a way to aggravate one of the neighbors. What the reason was, I'm not sure. Anyhow, we had the bright idea of collecting several large specimens of dog shit and depositing the same into our neighbor's mail box. Well, all hell broke loose when the mail man came on his daily route. It was damn near a federal case. Someone must have witnessed our "delivery", because we were quickly identified as the culprits and punishment was swift and painful.

21

I had my first "brush with the law" when I was ten years old. A new elementary school was under construction at the end of our block. With the piles of dirt, stacks of lumber, and partial structure, it was the perfect place for cowboys and Indians, king of the hill, hide-and-seek, and war games. The area had been declared off limits, and signs were posted indicating trespassers would be prosecuted. The consensus among my playmates was that we wouldn't have a problem if we waited until it was dark. It was winter time, and nightfall came early. One evening there were about ten of us having the time of our lives playing cowboys and Indians with the battleground encompassing the entire construction site. Suddenly, two police cars pulled up with lights flashing and panic set in. The game took a serious "life or death" turn, and we were shaking in our boots. Some of my buddies were apprehended straight off, while the rest of us took to hiding. I was not more than twenty yards from one of the police cars, and the cops were yelling for everyone to give themselves up. I pictured myself being carted off to jail, and was scared stiff. I stayed concealed for what seemed like an eternity, as the police scanned the area with their flashlights. Finally, the police left and I ran home. My parents asked where I'd been and I answered, "Oh, out playing cowboys and Indians."

An unforgettable incident happened to me when I was about twelve years old. I had been playing with a friend who lived at the other end of our block, and was on my way home. I was about to cross the street in front of his home, when a car crossed over to the curb and stopped in front of me. The driver, an unfamiliar man, leaned toward me and asked where a particular street was. I had never heard of the street he was inquiring about, which immediately made me uneasy. I knew most of the streets, especially at our end of town. He started talking with me like we were old friends, and was asking lots of questions. I told him I had to get home as my parents were expecting me. He reached across the seat opening the door on the passenger's side, and wanted me to get in his car with him. Mom and Dad had impressed on me never to accept a ride from a stranger. At that moment, my system was on "red alert" and the flight mechanism was set. I told the man I lived just a few houses down the street and thanked him anyway. He was still insistent and started to move toward me. I said no thanks and took off for home. I ran into our house and finally found dad in the backyard. I told him what had happened, and he came out front with me. Looking up and down the street, I saw the man in the car talking with another man on the sidewalk. He seemed to be with the man in the car and was pointing at me. They both had dark complexions and black hair. The car was only three houses away from us. When they saw my dad, the other man got in the car and they drove off. I never saw them again, but have wondered who they were and what they wanted. Over the years I conjectured they might have been contacts from the other side of my life. The thought was fascinating. Something like an extraterrestrial encounter. I remember that the man in the car had a warm friendliness about him and was persistent about talking with me. However, I can't imagine that it was an attempted kidnapping and was probably just a person who was lost looking for an address. Whenever I thought about my unknown past, that incident would come into mental focus.

For about six years, until I was fourteen, I took piano lessons. Boy, did I hate to practice. My parents expected me to spend an hour a day at the piano, and I did everything to sabotage that requirement. That was when I learned to lie about when and how long I'd practiced, so I could get out and play. At best, I was just a fair pianist and never had the virtuoso talent my mother just knew I had. Whenever relatives or close friends came to visit I was expected to perform. I invariably got rave reviews. As all of use have done at one time or another I have thanked my folks a thousand times for insisting I pursue the piano. Music is necessary for my well being, and to create my own, such as it is, has been their gift to me.

Unc drove up and stayed with us over weekends once or

twice a month. He was well-traveled, and had lived a full life at a relatively young age. He had spent time in Europe during the Second World War, and told me many stories about his experiences. A favorite story I had him tell me many times related to an incident which happened in London. He and a fellow officer were taking a walk through a district of London they had never seen before. Suddenly the strangest feeling came over him and he motioned for his friend to stop. Unc told his friend that even though he had never set foot on this street or been at this place in his life, he was experiencing an unexplainable phenomenon at that very moment. He had entered some kind of extrasensory dimension which made everything they were seeing completely familiar to him, as though he had lived there sometime during his life. He described to his friend in infinite detail what they would find down the next street and half block away. It was a little narrow side street with row houses and four or five retail establishments. He described the kinds of shops and houses, complete with colors, sizes, shapes, sign verbiage, and their exact locations on the street. His description was correct in every way. Unc never offered an explanation, other than to admit life is full of mysteries.

Three or four times a year, especially before Christmas, my folks and I would make a long jaunt into Los Angeles to shop at several of Mom's favorite department stores: The May Company, Bullock's, Robinson's, and Silverwood's. Several times I asked them if we could go by the Children's Home, where we became a family that eventful New Year's Day in 1943. My parents were always going to take me by, but we never seemed to find time. On our trip, there was a part of the drive that I looked forward to. Just before reaching the downtown area we went by a city park with a small picturesque lake that beckoned me. It was as if I'd been there before, much like Unc's London experience. Recently the answer came. My natural mother had taken me there many times as a young child.

I was baptized and confirmed in the Episcopal Church

and was an altar boy all through my boyhood. My parents rarely missed going to church on Sundays or the holidays during the year. Except when I had altar boy duties, we sat in the same pew for as long as I can remember.

I attended Harvard Military, an Episcopalian Church School in North Hollywood for several years. I boarded during the week and came home on weekends, except when I had to work off demerits. I was in good company. I went to school with, and knew the sons of Doris Day, Robert Mitchum, Richard Carlson, and Dan Duryea. Unc was member of the faculty at the time.

Being a military academy we had "dress blue" parades once a month or so. They were extravagant affairs. Parents came and watched the cadet battalion march around the parade grounds from the packed grandstand. I played the trombone in the corps band which provided march music for those military festivities.. I was also a member of the drill team. We occasionally performed as part of the program. We twirled, flipped and tossed our rifles into the air while marching in close-order drill. To this day it still amazes me that we made it through those performances without injury.

In the evenings before supper, we went to chapel for a short service. The church was beautiful and quaint, designed in the English tradition with pews facing across from one another. Once a week, at Evening Song, we could select our favorite hymnal songs and I invariably chose the same number, the Liturgy from St. James, which happened to be the priests' favorite as well, so we sang it often.

While at Harvard I continued being an altar boy. The duties were considerably more involved than at my hometown church. We were expected to lay out the priests' vestments just so, and set up the sacraments the night before the morning service. The sacraments consisted of bread and wine, and we had access to them so we could complete our preparations. One night a fellow altar boy suggested we take a "nip". I told him that was sacrilegious. He argued that the wine hadn't been blessed. He was sure we wouldn't go to Hell. It didn't take much persuasion. I joined him for a sip. After that, I rather looked forward to those evening preparations.

One of the subjects I studied while at Harvard was Latin. It was probably my most demanding class. I hated it. Languages and I never did get along. To make matters worse, my professor loved to torment me. I knew I was going to get called on regularly to recite, as one of my weaknesses was pronunciation. He was fond of calling me "Old Marblehead". My classmates loved it. I must say, the one thing I learned from his class was how to recite the Lord's Prayer in Latin, which I can do to this day.

Thirty years later I would discover that there was a young chap who attended Harvard at the same time, with whom I had alot in common. I didn't know him as he was several years younger and didn't stay long at the school. He was a link to my mysterious past. As destiny would have it, we were like brothers, yet as distant as heaven is from hell—for awhile we had the same mother.

My parents gave me the opportunity to find my interests. They must have spent a fortune on private lessons for tap dance, Cotillion, piano, trombone, swimming and tennis. I played the trombone in school and civic bands, and was on the tennis team for my high school. I have always enjoyed one-on-one competition, and cherish to this day a tennis trophy my team presented me in my senior year inscribed "Most Competitive". I played football in school, but wasn't tough or mean enough to be any good. In fact I played a little of all sports during my school days.

I mowed about eight lawns to get spending money, and eventually I bought my first car, a 1939 Chevy Coupe, with my savings. My dad helped me buy stocks, and in a year I doubled my investment. I've never done as well since!

I worked as a soda-jerk for several years. I pulled sodas at a place called the Blue Onion. I was fifteen years old when I first got the job in the summer of '56. It was a typical 50's drive-in, very much like the one in *American Graffiti*. It was the place everyone went after cruising, dragging, sporting events and dating.

Not long after I had been hired, a tough-looking guy approached me and asked when I was going to sign-up. "Sign-up for what?" I asked. I got a fifteen minute lecture on the benefits of being a member of Local #2896, the Bartenders and Culinary Arts Union. He said he'd be around again and I'd better join if I knew what was good for me! I eventually became a "Teamster" because my boss said things could get rough for me if I didn't.

Restaurant people are a hard-working lot. It's a backbreaking business. Generally speaking, the waitresses and cooks who worked at the Blue Onion had seen a lot of life and had been brought up in an environment foreign to me. That first summer at the Blue Onion was a real eye opener.

I worked there the following summer when I was sixteen and was driving my '39 Chevy Coupe. I had been given a raise and was working nights. My mom wasn't exactly happy about my working nights and would sometimes be "reading" when I came home about one-thirty in the morning or so.

The waitresses were a friendly group and enjoyed teasing me. They knew I was naive. I tried to act like a man-of-the-world, since I was big for my age, but they knew better. They were attractive and ranged in age from eighteen to twenty-five. Those who waited on the cars outside seemed to have a spirit all their own, and were called carhops—a close-knit group.

Gradually, over a three or four week period, I seemed to be getting the attention of one of the carhops. She was flirting with me, seductively. She was a young divorcee. I'd put it out of my mind, reasoning that it was just my imagination, but then I'd get a fetching wink, stare, or smile. She was cute, about 5' 5", and very attractive. When she walked, the sway of her rounded hips damn near drove me wild. Her breasts pressed against her white blouse, revealing that nature hadn't short-changed her there. She had auburn hair, that was cut short, blue eyes, and a pretty little sensual mouth. Her name was Cindy.

Why did I strike her fancy? she was at least two years older than I. She would subtly brush by me, giving my body a sensual taste. Her warm touch sent electric shocks straight to my loins. Whenever she called in a drink order, she would lean forward just enough for a marvelous view of her beautiful breasts. I tried very hard not to stare. It seemed this was a tease game she and her associates had concocted. My sexual hydraulic system worked overtime. When was this charade to end?

The other carhops knew what was happening. Occasionally one would say to me, "Cindy is hot for you. When are you going to ask her out?" I figured they said that to watch me blush, because I did. These waitresses were something else. Their enjoyment was at my expense, but I really didn't mind.

Cindy was fascinated with my hands. They were larger than average with long tapering fingers. One day while I was in the storeroom getting supplies for the fountain, she came to me complaining of a headache and wanted her neck massaged. I obliged. Cindy loved it and started slowly backing into me with her hips. Soon she was in contact with my groin area, and a certain part of my body was becoming hard and rigid. I was embarrassed, and backed off saying I had to get back to work. She just smiled, and thanked me for my services. For a week things got back to normal and the heat seemed to be off. Maybe she'd found herself a boyfriend her own age. I was starting to wish I'd had the guts to do something about all those lost opportunities.

One night after we had closed, Cindy came over while I was cleaning the fountain, and asked if I could give her a ride home. I couldn't believe my ears. The heat was on! She was apologetic, saying the girlfriend she'd been staying with had borrowed her car for some kind of emergency. I nervously looked around to see if any of her carhop friends were available to give her a ride. Not one of them was there. Being a gentleman I said, "Sure."

I spent an extra fifteen minutes cleaning up so that I

could pull myself together. After I ran out of things to clean, we walked out to my Chevy. It was about twelve twenty in the morning. I opened the door and she slid in. As I drove off, I asked her where she lived. "Down by the beach," she said.

Her perfume was having its effect on me, and I bashfully glanced toward her. My God, she had unbuttoned her blouse and was easing it off. "Watch where you're driving," I reminded myself. She unhooked her bra and let it fall. She softly kissed my neck and ear as her tantalizing breasts caressed my arm. Finally she pointed to a duplex, and I pulled into the carport. My car windows steamed up quickly. She shyly guided my hands to her womanliness and as I explored them with my fingers her nipples grew erect. She gently pulled my head to her bosom and I was going nearly insane. I'd been on dates before, but they were never like this! She placed her hand on my thigh and ever so slowly inched it to my zipper delicately opening my pants. Her fingers tenderly grasped my fully extended and aroused member as though scrutinizing its capacity to fulfill her carnal appetite. Her desire quickened to fever pitch. I undid the snaps on her jeans and pulled her jeans and panties down over her hips in one slow motion. She had repositioned herself in front of me and I was kissing her breasts and neck while caressing her smooth round hips with my hands. My God, was her body beautiful! Fine beads of moisture glistened over her body and gave off an erotic scent. I was close to ravishing and consuming her. While I roamed over her hips and thigh with one hand, the other was gently caressing and sensing every curve and crease from her supple breasts, down her body to her opening between her thighs. Cindy's breathing crescendoed to whimpering pants. Her body began undulating with a hypnotic rhythm that begged satisfaction, and at the same time she moved her leg around to place me in position.

I was about to enter her when suddenly I recoiled. My ardor was replaced by gripping fear, and I asked her to stop. Whether it was fear of what people, especially my parents, would think if they ever found out, or fear of inadequate performance, I can't say. Cindy was shocked and hurt. She wanted to know what was wrong. I told her it wasn't her fault, I just wasn't ready. She put her clothes on, and I walked her to the door of her apartment. I told her I was sorry and left. Mom didn't wait up for me that night. Thank God!

Such was my first experience with the act that leads to the creation of us all. I would find that my own conception occurred under similar conditions and circumstances—the product of impetuous passion. Life grabs hold where and when it can and mine hung by a mere thread.

I've often wondered how I was able to override that strongest natural body function, the desire to plant the seed of life. Parts of my body ached for lack of release. I worried for days wondering if I'd irreparably damaged my sexual delivery system. Over time, my concerns were put to rest.

I preferred objectivity over subjectivity; math and sciences over humanities. I could never understand or appreciate the beauty of literature or the need to refine communicative skills other than to know English grammar. It wasn't until much later in my life, when it came to me that the emotions, feelings, and thoughts of others appealed to my sensitivities. The whole world opened to me—Shakespeare, Byron, Keats, Shelley, Emerson, and others. The same authors I had read in school "per force", I now read, hanging onto the emotion and meaning of each word. Still, I have a love for thought-provoking games such as chess, bridge, backgammon and poker. I remember playing chess many summer evenings with my good friend who lived next door.

He was the same friend who was my partner in the lawn enterprise. We took on jobs that were next to impossible. One time we contacted a real estate office and asked if they had any properties to which we could apply our lawn-care skills, and were directed to a residence on the far side of town that had been vacant for some time. We had seen all states of lawn conditions, but this was a nightmare. The weeds in the backyard were unbelievable. No exaggeration, the weeds were as tall as we. It was a small area, but it took us all day and many blisters and thorny stab wounds before we finished. We looked like we had been in a bloody fight when we finally got home that night. As I recall, we were paid twenty dollars, ten each for our services. We never solicited work from that employer again.

We set up a telegraph system between our adjacent homes and sent Morse Code messages to each other for hundreds of hours when all we had to do was yell across the fence. We rode our bikes all over the county on butterfly hunts and visited post offices to get plate blocks for our stamp collections. We played quiz games for hours on end, and fantasized about how we could take over the world. He eventually went on to Yale, and was best man at my wedding.

There was a German family who moved in down the block from us. The father was a well-known scientist who came to the U.S. after World War II. There was a boy and two girls in the family. I became good friends with the boy. He taught me the game of chess and got me interested in chemistry. I had a chemistry set, and was fascinated with brewing acid. My bedroom was also my lab. It often smelled like sulfur or chlorine. My successes were evident by the various places that had been eaten away.

My bedroom was much more than a lab or place to lay my head. It was a private and cozy niche where I labored over homework, held trombone practice and listened to music. Above all it was a place where I could be by myself, which my parents respected and understood. I loved music and played my hi-fi for endless hours. Sometimes I'd play my horn along with Si Zentner, Don Shirley, Stan Getz, or Tommy Dorsey, and the neighborhood kids would come listen at my window. My corner of the house pulsated with the sounds of Elvis Presley, Fats Domino, Little Richard, Bill Haley and the Comets, Jerry Lee Lewis, the Everly Brothers, Johnny Mathis and Brenda Lee. I was particularly addicted to the primitive beat and sensuous rhythm-and-blues quality of Elvis Presley's music. The curious thing about Elvis was, that in a twisted and artificial way, destiny would link our lives and he would become a strange part of my "other life."

Nightmares were a frequent, unwelcome experience throughout my childhood, and were especially prevalent in the early years following my adoption. My parents were beside themselves with worry about what was causing the disturbing dreams. Mom had situated night lights at various locations, hoping that their glow would be reassuring and quiet my night time fears. Being pushed or thrown and falling helplessly through space to my death was a recurring theme. I have read that falling is not an uncommon plot of children's nightmares, but mine would come night after night. Calm, logical talks with me about my "unfounded" fear of falling didn't seem to help. Mom came when she heard me cry out, and would often change my sheets and PJ's that were drenched with my cold sweat. Often, I would lie in bed, afraid to go to sleep. Sometimes I would try to coax my dreams into a more comfortable story line. As the events of my past have unfolded, the reason for those "death fall" nightmares has come to light. In mid November, 1942, a very real incident, fraught with terror, sent me to a Los Angeles hospital emergency room, slamming the door shut on my past.

Belonging

Family secrets didn't stay secret long in our town. The fact that I was adopted rarely came up as a discussion topic. It was something that was tucked away and not mentioned. The few times the subject surfaced I was somewhat uncomfortable. I wanted so much to have others believe that these people I lived with and loved as parents, were in fact my natural father and mother. No matter how hard I tried, the truth would not change. Mother nature helped me see my folly. As I grew older, it became more and more obvious from my physical appearance that my biological genesis was not from them.

Physically, I was the size of my parents when I was thirteen years old. I had a dark complexion with black hair and blue eyes. By the time I was eighteen, I was 6'1" and weighed over two hundred pounds. With a slow metabolism and the love of food, especially spicy, hot dishes, I had to watch my weight. Dad ate more than I and always stayed thin.

The reality that I was adopted was ever with me, but I buried that fact very deep within. My mom and dad were very private people, especially Mom. When they told me of my adoption, I knew it was a very personal and sensitive piece of information. It was our family secret. At the same time, I realized it was likely all my friends knew our secret before I did. They came from families who had lived in my hometown for many years. Back then, the transient population of Oxnard was small.

Since there was a good chance my peers either knew or would find out about my situation, that probably prompted my parents to tell me. I've often wondered how hard it was for them to tell me I was adopted. How long did they debate and agonize over the issue? Surely that was a traumatic moment in their lives.

At the time they told me, I was in the third grade. Part of their decision had to be when to tell me. I was very young, and they took the chance that I might not be able to handle such a formidable secret. On the other hand, there was the possibility that I might hear it from a third party.

I know now, that regardless of when young people are told of their adoption it is a heavy weight to carry. It was for me. Thirty-eight years ago, society was less tolerant of individual differences—today such a disclosure might be easier. In the early 1950's, American society had a compulsion to identify and place people into neat ideological categories. McCarthyism was on the move, and you belonged or you didn't.

I've always had a strong desire for belonging and peer acceptance, which isn't uncommon during youth. Knowing that I was adopted, I perceived I was different from my peers. That secret had to be guarded at all costs. It was absolutely unthinkable for me to have casually mentioned to a childhood friend that I was adopted. I imagined he would have said to himself, "You've got to be kidding. What kind of freak are you!?"

The chance of a kid saying, "Well, isn't that great, you got to choose your parents, how lucky you are," was near zero. That wasn't just my perception, but probably reality in those days. Children are brutally honest. At that time the reality for me was that I didn't share the flesh, blood and God-knew-what-else with my parents.

I dearly loved my parents, and we were very close to each other. My attempted solution was to make people believe these adults were my natural parents. My ordeal was not all-encompassing but enough to cause reticence and even withdrawal, if there was a chance I'd be in the limelight. I couldn't take the risk of someone discovering that I was different from my parents. The less time they had for comparison the better.

Even with immediate family relatives or very close friends, I was guarded. Occasionally the subject would surface in their presence and I sensed strange, alienating stares my way. That was a figment of my negative imagination, but nevertheless it was real to me. I buried the fact, and was extremely defensive.

When I was in the sixth grade one of my classmates let me know he knew my secret. He wasn't one of my friends, and was an antagonistic sort. I think he realized I would have taken him apart if he ever opened his mouth. He never did openly divulge my secret as far as I knew, but the fear that he would was ever with me. I stayed clear of him, for I feared he would blackmail me for all I had.

My mother taught at the same elementary school I went to from the first through sixth grades. Having a mother as a school teacher was something like being a preacher's kid. Subconsciously, my peers probably thought favoritism came my way. That certainly wasn't the case! There were several times I remember being taken to the principal's office for deserved spankings. Mom heard about it later, and I caught it again at home. That was double jeopardy! If only my friends knew my fate. I never regretted having a school teacher as my mom. She was well-respected and known throughout our town.

During my years at home I knew other adopted children. My mother tried to let me know who they were—that I wasn't alone. I studied and watched them carefully. Now that I think about it, I dwelt on it too much. I detected peculiarities and labeled them "different," when in fact the "genetic"—kids had some of the same peculiarities. However, there were apparent similarities among adopted children that couldn't be rationalized away.

I had a good friend who was almost like a brother during my early years. His mother was a school teacher, and was a close friend of Mom's—we lived on opposite sides of town, which meant that when we got together, we usually stayed at each other's home a night or two. We played cards and board games and outside we played cars and trucks. We made elaborate water systems in the dirt like rivers and lakes for hours on end. His father was a farmer and brought home lots of fresh fruit and vegetables. We both had a taste for green onions, and in-between meals we had his specialty—green onion sandwiches. They were delicious and great for our breath! When I visited his home I was part of the family. I loved them all.

My friend had an older brother who was different in many ways. Even though he physically resembled my friend's father, the brother's emotional makeup, mentality and character came from somewhere else. I sensed it in the early years. It was neither good or bad, just distinct. I liked him, but could never quite put my finger on why he seemed peculiar to me. It wasn't until I was fifteen, Mom told me my friend's brother was adopted. That possibility never occurred to me. Then I understood! His parents had thought having children of their own wasn't possible and so they adopted a son, and had the surprise of their lives several years later when my friend was born to them.

After that, I wondered if I seemed strange to others. Did I appear to be part of the fabric of my family, or was it obvious that I was a flaw in the pattern? I had an overwhelming desire to "belong," and not be an outsider. Kids sense when one is pushing to belong and acceptance becomes more difficult. I was never one to require a multitude of friends. I liked having a few good friends to know and enjoy as completely as I could.

There was a boy just down the street who was also adopted. His mom and dad were nice people. They were genteel, kind and respected folks. He was the opposite, almost from a different planet. He was forever getting into fights; he was loud, boisterous, uncouth and in general a jerk. Seeing a police car in front of his house with lights flashing was not unusual. On one occasion I found out he had declared war on his neighbors, and had been shooting "flaming arrows" onto roof tops! I felt sorry for his parents. What went wrong? Was it in his genes? Could his adopted mom and dad have changed him? I don't think so. How much of a persons' character is inherited? Maybe I would find out some day.

My "adoption" became sensitive just a few times during my youth. One time I was outside my home playing with three of my friends. I was having an argument with one, and in a fit of anger he yelled, "Well anyhow, you don't even know who your real parents are, you're nothing but a bastard!" I became an instant madman. I was furious. My friend was bigger and one year older than me, but at that moment he could have been a champion boxer. I didn't care. My rage was such that I'm afraid I would have seriously hurt him if I hadn't been stopped. He was bleeding from the nose and mouth. That was a feeling I've had few times in my life. My friend never brought it up again.

Once my piano teacher, who didn't know I was adopted, commented that one of her pupils acted strange, and hinted that it was because he was adopted. I didn't say anything, but it bothered me—it hurt. Other adopted children that I knew of seemed to have a common lack of self-confidence—probably caused by the fear of someone asking, "Who are you?"

Mom and Dad introduced me to as many relatives as possible from each side of the family. I never lacked for a family background. I knew most of my relatives very well and loved them all as they loved me. My parents made sure I was aware of and understood my family heritage. I felt like a member of the family—a Deatherage.

Years later, when I had my own family and lived in Virginia, Dad came out for a visit. While there, he wanted to visit the old Deatherage plantation in Culpepper County, founded by his ancestors from England. We were living in Burke at the time, and it took about an hour to get to the general area near Front Royal. Dad didn't know exactly how to get to the Deatherage homestead, so we asked at a little store. Several people overheard and were anxious to help direct us. It was a well-known landmark. It was called Horseshoe Farm.

When we arrived there was an impressive structure, but

the style was different than I had expected. I had pictured a colonial plantation house, something out of *Gone With the Wind*. Instead of being a rectangular two-story structure, it rambled as though there had been many additions over its 250 years. Native stone was used rather than brick. The people who owned it gave us a tour of the main house and slave quarters.

Whenever I'm in a historical place like that, I think about the generations of people who lived and died there. The collection of human experiences captured within those walls would have filled several books. I almost expected a Deatherage ghost to whisper something to me.

We went out behind the slave quarters, and there nestled under giant oak trees was the old family cemetery. Deatherages have been resting there since the 1700's. We quietly read names, dates and sometimes there were inscriptions. I looked up and noticed that my wife seemed to be frozen in front of a headstone. I walked over and followed her gaze. She was staring down at a grave which had her name, Susan F. Deatherage, Died 1832—a subtle reminder of our mortality.

Just as I was getting warm, contented feelings about our family historical discovery, it occurred to me that these Deatherages weren't my ancestors. My genes and blood came from a different stock. My thrill of history was in name only. Dad loved the visit and the communion with his ancestors.

For years now, I have had regular medical physicals. The doctor would discuss my medical history with me. He'd ask about immediate family members; father, mother, brothers, and sisters. I'd give him my adopted family status as I was hesitant about divulging that I was adopted. Father: living, in good health. Mother: deceased June 1965, heart attack. Siblings: none. Finally, these past several years I decided it wasn't doing me any good to fake it. I simply told the doctor, "I'm adopted." He, in turn, silently wrote in the family history block, "UNKNOWN."

My wife reminds me I never mentioned that I was adopted until we had dated for sometime. I remember the situation well. We had been getting fairly serious about each other, and I was waiting for an appropriate time to propose marriage. There was this thing about being adopted that I needed to tell her. I had never volunteered that personal piece of information to anyone in my twenty-two years. It took me several weeks before I could find the courage. How would she react? Would I lose her? It was like admitting that I had some kind of disease. In this case it was called "not knowing who I am," which I would be passing on to our children. My anxiety level was at fever pitch, the night I told her. I was very nervous, and it was all I could do to mutter, "Susan, I think you should know I'm adopted." To my surprise, her reaction was, "So what's the problem?" We talked about it for a while, and I told her what I knew. What a relief that was, and I tucked it away again. If she had realized the events that would take place twenty-four years later, and the eventual typing demands of this project, she would have thought twice.

Several years ago, David, my oldest son, visited my folks over a long weekend. I was happy Dave had a chance to be with his grandfather. Dad wrote to say how much they enjoyed him with them, and what a great time they had together. We hadn't heard from David, but I visited him not long afterwards. We weren't together ten minutes when David gave me a rather disgusted look and said, "Why didn't you tell me you were adopted?" I didn't know what to say and the silence was deafening.

Finally, I said, "I'm sorry, David. All my life that personal piece of information has been a hard subject for me to talk about. . . . How did it come up?"

David replied, "We were trying to decide which restaurant to go to for dinner and Grandpa commented, 'If Gary were here we'd be eating Italian or Mexican food—it's that Italian blood in him.' " David continued, "I must have looked surprised because Gramps quickly added, 'You know we adopted your dad when he was 18 months old.' I nodded like I knew it. By the way, Dad, we went to a Mexican restaurant."

I said, "I'll bet Gramp's revelation caught you off balance. Did it bother you?"

"Yeah, it surprised me alright," Dave replied, "but it really didn't bother me . . . except . . . why didn't you tell me about it before?"

After a long pause, I said, "It was a family secret for so long that I buried it too deep within myself to tell anybody. Your mom is the only one I've told—it's hard to explain. . . ." David seemed to understand. I soon realized there just wasn't a good reason, and that I owed it to my sons to tell them. What fate had dealt out for me, was their inheritance as well. I gave Dave all the background information I knew about myself at the time. The fact that I was adopted didn't seem to bother him, which I understood, since he was a generation removed from the genetic implications.

Not long after my visit with David, I had a father-to-sons talk with John and Mike, telling them I was adopted and relating what I knew about my history. They were very quiet and I could sense they were going to need a few minutes to sort things out. I remember wishing I had made my confession years ago. I supposed their immediate dilemma focused on "Gramps". How did the unfolding of this secret affect their relationship with him? They loved him dearly, and they certainly knew I did. Would this change their feelings toward him? I'm ashamed, but happy to admit I had underestimated their maturity. Of course, Gramps was Gramps and they would always love him! They appeared only mildly concerned about the change in their genetic inheritance. Like David, they knew who their natural father was and beyond that it was only academic.

It was harder to tell my sons of my adoption than I thought it would be. It wasn't quite like discussing an everyday problem with them. I could feel a tug from deep within. I felt a loneliness and vulnerability as I exposed a very personal part of me. Why would I feel that way with my own sons? That was ridiculous! I had buried that secret so deep and so long because of fear—fear that I would be considered different and an outcast if my adoptedness became known—fear that my sons would take on my hang-up, the question of belonging.

Coming Of Age

In 1959 I went off to school at the University of Oregon in Eugene. My college years were undoubtedly one of the best periods of my life. A time filled with many good friends, happy times, and above all, the ingredients to find and understand myself. I joined a fraternity and had all the brotherhood I missed as an only child. My biological beginnings and the mysterious first eighteen months of my life rarely came to mind.

My mom had told me for as long as I could remember that I was destined to become a doctor. I went off to school all set to become the family's first G.P. I enrolled in Pre-Med. I had done well in sciences and math in high school, and figured it would be a breeze. I had a rude awakening—it was tough. Besides the academic pressure, I pledged Delta Tau Delta Fraternity and matriculated in three other courses; partying, dating and bridge. It took me two years and mediocre grades to realize that doctors were made of sterner stuff. I changed to economics and math, and transferred to another school. I managed to get my degree and eventually went to work on an MBA at the University of Utah.

During my pre-med days, there were several courses which discussed biological and environmental effects. Which was dominant? I studied how genes determined physical likeness with parents, not only in exterior appearances, but also included gland, brain and nervous system similarities. I learned that environment creates a value basis—values being things learned, opinions formed, and traditions accepted. Needless to say, I found such topics stimulating. I could certainly attest to the environmental aspect, but my biological heritage remained blank.

When I thought about my biology class, it brought to mind an interesting story a friend shared with me about her life. Like myself, she had taken biology and recalled a discussion on dominant and recessive genetic traits. The professor was reviewing Gregor Mendel's discoveries on inherited dominant characteristics, and was commenting that dark hair and skin were dominant, just as brown eyes were over blue. When they went over various parental characteristics and the probable genetic outcomes, it was pointed out how rare it was for blue-eyed parents to have brown-eyed offspring. My brown-eyed friend enthusiastically volunteered to the class that she was one of those rare cases.

Several years later, when she was twenty, her father confessed that her natural mother died when she was a three month old baby, and that the mother she had always known was actually her stepmother. What a shock that must have been! Her natural mother had brown eyes. For some reason her dad never told her the truth about her birth until she was an adult. She had three brothers by her dad and stepmother, and remembered during childhood that at times family interrelationships seemed strained and incoherent. Over the years she sensed a difference between herself and her brothers, and after her father's revelation, she understood. She wished, however, that he had told her as a young girl. She said, "I've learned two things while taking the course of adulthood. Things are often not what they seem to be, and you are as psychotic as your secrets." I knew what she meant.

I transferred to Southern Oregon College (SOC) in the winter of 1961. The campus was located in the scenic little town of Ashland, which is situated in the foothills of the Siskiyou Mountains, just south of Medford. Back then, Ashland was a quaint college town, population 5,000. It was a quiet place, compared with the "big time" university life in Eugene. During those years at SOC, I played trombone for the college orchestra and band, and enjoyed it immensely. We had several concerts in the spring in Lithia Park.

Lithia Park was an absolutely beautiful place. The park was impeccably cared for by the city. Located in a narrow valley just off the Main Street, it stretched for two miles and was as much as one-half mile wide. There was a wide variety of tree and plant life, which were arranged by nature and man into an exquisite concert of majesty and color. The floor of the park was carpeted with luscious green grass. A babbling brook meandered from one end to the other. There were scenic ponds at each end where ducks and swans lived and prospered. Winding paths took the visitor into the depths of this paradise. A white band shell marked the spot where weekly concerts were held by the civic band. At the entrance to Lithia Park was the Ashland Shakespearean Theatre, well known and active from late spring until early fall.

Whenever I wanted time by myself to think or relax, I would go to Lithia Park. Its' cures were not unknown to me. The peaceful tranquility of that beautiful place made everything right in the world. I went there often.

During those years in Ashland I thought about my life quite often. Pulling all the parts together was a sobering and fascinating experience. That was the first time I had ever made an effort to really know who I am. It was as though I had been hiding from myself for twenty years. My identity was limited to the sum of my environment and experiences. That was when a spark from within ignited my desire to seek out from whence I sprang. The ember was small and only occasionally became hot over the years. There were so many compelling questions. Who were the man and woman that connected to form the human vessel I saw in the mirror each day? At the time, my knowledge of them was perfunctory at best. The only description my parents presented was: My natural mother came from English and German ancestry, was blonde and musically inclined; while my natural father was Italian and dark. From my folk's perspective, that explained their insistence for music lessons, my love of spicy foods, and my hot-blooded disposition.

I felt if only I knew my natural parents, I could better understand myself. I can remember lying on the cool grass in Lithia Park, trying to conjure up a picture of them. I tried to call up any speck of information from memory, but it was no use. The barrier to my past was impenetrable—I couldn't remember. Then, more questions would come. Why didn't they want me? Were they kind, gentle and loving? Are they dead? Did I have brothers and sisters? I knew the answers to these questions were far away, and reluctantly realized I might never unearth those secrets in this life.

Toward the end of my junior year I saw a poster in the student union building that told about summer employment at Crater Lake National Park. I didn't have a job lined up back home, and this opportunity seemed like an excellent respite. I signed up for an interview. They were only taking applications from college people, and quite a few at SOC signed up. An older gentleman was conducting the interviews, and we had a good visit. I told him my background, including the restaurant work, but he was most interested in my fraternity affiliation. It seems the owner's son was a Delt at Oregon State University. I was in! It was off to Crater Lake that last "free" summer of my life.

I had been to Crater Lake many years before with my parents. I remembered it as being a unique creation of nature. Nothing had changed, except there were a few new facilities to cater to the tourists. The main lodge, which had been built in the 1930's, was still there and was the place to stay at the lake. As lodges go, it was smaller than average. It was a tall narrow structure, which perched on the rim overlooking the lake. The lodge had a seasoned, inviting look about it. The evenings were cool, and burning logs in the large fireplace made the main room in the lodge comfortable, warm and cozy. It was built in the same traditional style of all the national park lodges of that era.

My job was to manage the soda fountain located in the cafeteria a block down from the lodge. All the employees were expected to help entertain the guests with whatever talents they had, and three evenings a week, I played the piano. The college help all resided in the main lodge on the fourth floor. There were probably one hundred college employees working there that summer, from schools all over Oregon. They were a diverse, fun group of young people. We even had several tables of bridge.

There was an incident that happened at the lake, which teased me for years. I was walking along the rim path, not far from the lodge, when suddenly a dark, middle-aged man broke away from his friends and rushed over, giving me a big hug, like we were long-lost relatives from the old country. He was very excited, almost in tears, and talked to me in a foreign language. He was about my height, medium build, with dark hair and eyes. Even though his overtures seemed genuinely friendly, almost paternal, I was taken aback and guarded. His face reflected a multitude of expressions in rapid succession; delight, surprise, contemplation and love. It was obvious he had mistaken me for someone else—or had he? One of his friends came over and explained in broken English that I looked and acted exactly like this man's nephew, who lived in America. They were Italian. The thing that was curious, even after I explained who I was, was that the man was still convinced I was his nephew. His eyes followed me after we parted. Many times over the years I wished I had at least asked his name.

Crater Lake was mysterious to me. The lake itself is several hundred feet down from the rim and out of reach, except by hiking down to it. The lake could be seen, but one could not readily touch it. It was silent. I never heard waves lapping the shore, or any water sounds at all. The only sound was a constant breeze rustling through the pines at the rim. When there was no moon or breeze, it was completely black and absolutely quiet. It was like being on another planet—a solitary feeling. At night I frequently wondered what was happening down on the lake. It was a subconscious uneasiness that I couldn't explain. It was out

47

of reach, just like my past.

During the day, the lake was the deepest blue imaginable. The lake is nearly 2,000 ft. deep, which makes it the deepest lake in the United States. I went around the rim many times that summer and knew all the best vantage points. Crater Lake had a stark beauty about it. At night, when there was a full moon, it was gorgeous. The moonlight was so illuminating, I often drove with my headlights off. The reflection of the moonbeams off the lake was a blinding silver streak.

Before I knew it, that summer was only memories. A few snow flurries rudely announced that fall had come. The employees had a farewell party, and we closed up the lodge for the winter.

One day that fall I was in the SOC Student Union, having a Coke with a friend and happened to notice a cute, young lady who was working in the Snack Bar. Judging by the innocent glow about her, she was a freshman. On closer observation, she was not only cute, but pretty. She was about 5'7", with auburn hair, blue eyes and had a nice figure. She had on a tan skirt and a brown autumn-colored sweater. When she walked, she swayed back and forth to her own music. I knew right away I had to meet her. I asked my friend if he knew who she was, and he said no, but he wanted to find out.

The next Friday night a school dance was on my "things to do" list. Normally I avoided school dances, but I knew she'd be there. The minute I walked in I saw her with several other girls, and immediately walked over. My eyes met hers and I asked her to dance. We danced under the glittering, rotating silver ball that sent colorful reflections over the dance floor and swayed to the music of Johnny Mathis, Nat King Cole, Tony Bennett, Paul Revere and the Raiders, and others. Her name was Susan. We talked as we danced and enjoyed each other. When a slow number played, we danced close and her body felt good. As I held her close to me, the chemistry was right, and I knew she was the one I had been searching for. Susan married me on June 22, 1963 and eventually became the mother of my three sons. I graduated from SOC that same year.

Summer was spent before we knew it. I had applied for a special program to go to Artillery Officer Candidate School (OCS) at Fort Sill, Oklahoma, and was accepted. After New Year's, I flew to Oklahoma City and was bussed to Fort Sill, near Lawton, to begin OCS training. I had never been so cold! There were subfreezing temperatures most of January and February. I was allowed to see Susan two hours per week those first two months, and occasionally weekends in March and April, and finally on weekends from May until graduation in June. Those were trying times for us, except for one important event. On one of those weekends in May, our son David was conceived. When Sue told me, I was ecstatic, and as time passed, I watched and felt him grow in Susan. I remember wondering if my natural mother and father had the same feeling of joy at my conception. In a strange way, I fantasized that David's prenatal development and eventual birth was a reflection of what my own birth was like. Nobody discussed my birth with me. It was as if I had been hatched at the Children's Home when I was eighteen months old. Our David was due sometime the first part of February, 1965. I could hardly wait.

I seriously doubt I could have handled the insane truth about my birth back then. Even now, the reality of the circumstances in which I entered this life are repulsive to me. Instead of finding that my coming was pampered with love, it turns out quite the opposite. It was only through the grace of God that I was born into this world.

Graduation from OCS came none too early. My parents came for the ceremonies when my Second Lieutenant Bars were pinned on, and I was commissioned as an artillery officer in the U.S. Army. My first duty station was Fort Bliss, Texas, and I was to report there in three weeks. In the meantime, we went to Green Mountain Falls, Colorado, where I spent several weeks unwinding. Unc's family built a cabin there in the 1920's and I had spent many summers there as a boy. It was like going home, and I took Sue to all the favorite haunts. Before we knew it, the three weeks had flown by, and it was time to head off to our new home.

El Paso and nearby Fort Bliss were hot in the middle of July. As we approached El Paso, I told Susan, "What a God-forsaken place this is!" She agreed. El Paso's stark desert beauty didn't impress us, compared with the lush green of Oregon or Colorado. However, over time, our sensory perceptions changed dramatically, and we grew to love El Paso. I was assigned to Center Headquarters, and had a super Colonel for a boss. The office folks were a congenial close-knit group. Sue and I quickly settled into our on-post duplex, and developed close friendships with many of the young couples in our neighborhood. We still hear from some of them at Christmas time. We all had so many things in common. We were bridge players, just starting families, shave-tail second lieutenants, straight out of college, and we were party people. The military life was good for us in those days. Vietnam was just starting to stir.

On February 10, 1965, I witnessed the birth of a being that shared my genetics; our first son, David Gary, Jr. Mom and Dad came out in March to meet their new and only grandson. As it turned out, Mom came in the nick of time and seemed to really enjoy her grandmother status. She passed away rather suddenly in June of that same year. She died of a heart attack on her wedding anniversary. Her departure was an agonizing loss, and was the only time in my adult life that I broke down and wept. I loved her very much. On June 2, 1967, our son John Marcus was born, and on my birthday in 1970, our third son, Michael Floyd was born.

Each time I saw my sons for the first time, I would go over every square inch of their tiny bodies many times. The mystery of life was awesome. Most parents know what I'm saying and have experienced the same feeling. Mine was more. I was searching. My sons were clues to my ancestral past. Eventually, I knew they'd want to know their history too. They'd know my dad as their Gramps and would love him as I do. However, someday I'd tell them I was adopted and then they'd wonder as I have.

In April of 1966, I had to make a monumental decision. Should I stay in the military or go to the private sector? Military life had been good to us, but I decided to become a civilian. I accepted a position with General Dynamics in Fort Worth, Texas. It was difficult to bid farewell when we left Fort Bliss, and over the years I have occasionally had second thoughts about leaving the military. We arrived in Fort Worth in July after Susan' s graduation from Texas Western College. We found a little place not far from the plant where I went to work with 21,000 others. We were building the F-111 fighter aircraft for the Navy and Air Force. I was a cost accountant, keeping track of engineering research expenditures. Early the next year Dad gave me the box, and my destiny took a new turn.

In March, 1967, I accepted a position with the government, and was transferred to Wiesbaden, West Germany. I left the United States content with my new personal knowledge given up by the box. We lived in Germany for four and a half years. During that time, I occasionally pulled out the box and revisited its contents. But, being out of the United States, it was not conducive or practical to think about searching for my past. Life in Europe was full, and we took advantage of the opportunity to travel.

We started our new life in Germany in fine fashion. Sue gave birth to our second son the third month we were there. Months before John's birth, we had discussed at great length, possible names—be it boy or girl. If it was a girl, we liked the name Deborah Susan. If a boy, we both liked John, but couldn't decide on the middle name. It hadn't been long since finding out my birth name was Marcus Gary, so why not use Marcus? It seemed clever at the time, and the names, John Marcus sounded good together. A year after John was born, my folks visited us in Germany while on a tour in Europe. My stepmother got me aside, and asked why we gave John his middle name, Marcus. I was speechless. She proceeded to let me know that Dad knew where the name came from and was disappointed and hurt. Guilt consumed me, as I had not been sensitive to the feelings of my Dad. Somehow, I had discounted that he would even remember that my name was Marcus.

We lived in the American Arms, a transient hotel in Wiesbaden for the first three and a half months. We adjusted to our new life in no time. I had two years of German in college, which helped, and most Germans knew English. We grew to understand and enjoy the German people, their customs and traditions. We were in the heart of the German Rhineland and quickly developed a taste and appetite for wine, beer, pastries and wursts. It was impossible not to gain weight.

Our first home was in Bad Schwalbach, a very picturesque village located in the Taunus Mountains twenty miles from Wiesbaden. It was nestled in a little valley and the surrounding hills were covered with pine forests. We lived in a very large three-family apartment building. Our friends who told us about it lived in the upper apartment, and a German couple lived in the one below. The German was married to a young Chinese girl whose sister lived with them. We lived on the side of a hill and the view of our village and countryside was fantastic.

There is another view I remember well. Among other things, it was instructive about life in Europe. One afternoon, I was in our apartment, babysitting with John. Sue and David were out shopping. It was a sunny, warm afternoon. I heard some people talking in the backyard area. When I looked over our balcony, I was startled by a rather uncommon, but delightful scene. I had never seen our downstairs neighbors before, but I sure did this time. The two Chinese ladies were sunning themselves and were completely nude. They were lying on their stomachs with their heads up toward the apartment. When they heard me, they both raised up to give me a big smile and greeting. The married one was very petite, with extremely fine features. She was cute and her breasts and hips were appropriately shaped for her small body. Her sister was something else!

She had rounded, full breasts and hips which I hadn't thought were characteristic of Chinese women. With most Chinese women, those features had generally seemed unpretentious and not so pronounced. She had a very pretty face, with fine features like her sister. They both were in their early twenties, and had absolutely beautiful skin—radiant and smooth.

The petite, married one, got up and went inside her apartment. The sister stayed and slowly rolled over on her back. She had the shiniest black hair I've ever seen, and her waist was slender, accentuating her female parts. I knew right then I needed to get back inside. I was a married man. I wondered if our upstairs friends had ever seen this. After ten minutes or so, I ventured back out onto the balcony. She was sitting and positioned so that she was looking directly at me. I couldn't jump back. I was caught by her eyes. She motioned for me to come down onto the grass with her. I couldn't believe how forward she was, especially knowing I was a married family man. I told her no, and she just gave me a knowing, beckoning smile.

We moved that next summer (because of winter driving conditions—not the downstairs neighbors!) into a single family house in Ginsheim. Our home was within two blocks of the Rhine River, where we walked almost every evening. It was a family outing. David and I had many philosophical and world-event discussions during those walks. As we talked, barges moved silently by us, and occasionally we interrupted our conversation to greet Germans who passed us on the path. David was such a bright, delightful child. Our dog, Fred, had the time of his life. He was four years old then and loved running those river paths. Thank God for memories!

We found Germans to be logical and conservative people who want respect and authority. They like to have things neatly labeled and in their proper place. Their lives are highly structured from youth through adulthood. They work and play hard. When relaxing, Germans love to sing, eat and drink beer or wine, and have the time of their lives.

Many are chess players, and often when we went to city parks, there would be several games in progress.

Occasionally, with friends we would talk about Adolph Hitler, and whether a similar situation could happen today. The consensus was yes. Germans love a strong leader and their loyalty and dedication are unquestioned. They are a very traditional and prejudiced people. Shortly after John was born, our next door neighbor came to visit. She and Susan were good friends and both had new babies. Susan was changing John's diapers and her friend noticed that he had been circumcised. She scolded Susan and told her that circumcision was bad, and only Jews held to that practice. It was bad, because someone might get confused and think John was Jewish if a problem ever surfaced again. Susan and I were surprised that such an attitude persisted. In fact, the same couple confessed to be atheists, but had their son baptised anyway for future documentation. I suspect anti-Semitism is still subtly widespread in Germany and Europe.

We had a *putzfrau* (maid) whom we adored and she us. She was a sweet little old lady, who took care of us like we were her family. In fact, the kids called her "Tante" (aunt) Anna, and loved her. When Mike was born she looked after him as though he were her own. For many years after we left Germany, we continued to write "Tante" Anna and our other German friends at Christmas time.

We saw much of Europe in our four and a half years. We were all over Germany many times. We also went to Switzerland several times, and toured France, Italy, England, Berlin, Amsterdam, Austria, Holland and Luxembourg.

After learning I was being transferred to the Washington, D.C. area in November, 1971, I dusted off the box and revisited its contents. The urge to start my search took hold. I began thinking about checking phone directories and calling Information for a listing of an Andrew or Rebecca Kullberg. At the same time, there was a side of me that didn't want to find out any more about myself. I sensed a foreboding at what lay in wait for me at the other side of my life.

Once I remember Unc telling me that it would be best to keep the door to my past closed, because the chances of hurt and disappointment were much greater than happy discoveries. I realized there was much wisdom in his advice, but at the same time, I knew I would want to open that mysterious door someday.

The Search Begins

We flew into Dulles International Airport on Thanksgiving Eve, 1971. It was snowing and a beautiful sight. Our good friend, who had lived in the upstairs apartment in Bad Schwalbach, and who was now living in Fairfax, Virginia, met us. What a carload that was—Sue and our three sons, David, John and Mike, ages six, four and one; our poodle, Fred; and mounds of luggage. Our friend took us to Arlington where we stayed while we found a home. It wasn't long before we bought a townhouse in Burke, Virginia. Several weeks passed before we could move into our new home. With the extra time, I decided to make some phone calls. I was going on a "Kullberg" hunt. It couldn't do any harm, and besides, my curiosity was building.

A weekend before we moved, I became acquainted with the AT&T information operators in the Virginia, District of Columbia and Maryland areas. This was my first "search" effort. I spent two or three hours on the phone, and talked with about twelve different information operators. I got a half-dozen phone numbers with the initials A or R to go with Kullberg. No listings for Rebecca or Andrew. None of the phone calls netted me an Andrew or Rebecca either, or leads to them. I would ask if they knew of an Andrew or Rebecca Kullberg. The answer was usually an immediate "no." Once in a while, I'd get a "Why do you want to know?" I'd explain, "They were close family friends many years ago," and then the "no" would come. It was disappointing, but I had expected the going to be long and tedious.

In a way, I was relieved when I failed in those early years. Searching on the West Coast had the best prospects and I believe my efforts in the east were subconscious attempts to guarantee failure. Even though I wanted to open that mysterious door, I just wasn't ready or mature enough to handle the consequences. If I made contact, would I be able to cope with facing the "other side"? I tried to picture what it would be like. Could I deal with the responsibility of bringing my natural mother and father back to life, when they had been dead to me? What horrors would I find? I was a conservative, traditional and faithful person. Would a discovery break the faith with my Dad, who I had always known and loved? There was a spiritual bond between us that I didn't want to jeopardize. Could I keep my sanity? Would it be a nightmare? All this against knowing the truth. The stakes were high, but the gamble seemed worth it.

In January we moved into our new home, which was our first to own. Burke was situated in Fairfax County and not more than a wide spot in the road. Our development, Burke Station Square, was nestled in the woods of the Virginia countryside, and was a suburban oasis in the hectic Washington, D.C. metropolitan area. Our townhouse had a garage and storage-utility room on street level, with living areas that accessed our backyard on the second floor, and bedrooms on the third. The facade was red brick and the style, English traditional, as were the other homes in the neighborhood. In the spring, we put window boxes on the street side, and Sue loaded them with colorful geraniums in German fashion. At our end of Kara Place, the street was divided by a large island, which had tall beautiful oak trees, where our boys liked to play. We had never lived in the East, and like Germany, found nature's four seasons a feast for the senses.

The secrets of my past would eventually lead me to the East. To New York City, where my natural grandfather met his end. His Sicilian birth and acquaintance with Al Capone put him in heavy company.

To commute to 14th Street in downtown D.C. took thirty-five to forty minutes. I carpooled for a year or so with other government civilians who worked in the District.

There was a fellow who worked for the Social Security Administration that I got to know and became friends with. Part of his job was searching for people for one reason or another. Once I asked how difficult it would be to find a person, given only a name. He said it would be difficult on a national basis, but not too bad by state, and if a social security number was available, then no problem at all. I debated whether to ask my friend for the favor of locating Andrew or Rebecca Kullberg, but put it off, and he eventually left the D.C. area. I kicked myself later, wishing I'd pursued it with him.

As we approached our two year anniversary in Virginia, my family and I were enjoying life to the fullest. In fall of 1973, I noticed a very small growth on my arm, which looked like a pimple, but was beet red. It occasionally itched, but that was all. The thing that bothered me was that it stayed the same for at least five weeks. I had my doctor examine it and he casually said, "It's nothing, but I recommend it be removed," which he did. Several days later he called me at my office and said he wanted to see me that afternoon, as soon as possible. I asked him what the problem was and he put me off until our visit.

I sat down in his office, and he looked at me and said, "I don't believe in beating around the bush. I'm afraid you have a malignant melanoma."

I asked, "What's that?"

He replied, "Skin cancer."

What a shock that was! He said that he had taken the liberty of lining me up with a surgeon who specialized in skin cancer techniques. He had made the hospital arrangements for the earliest date possible, which was in four days. Time was of the essence. The procedure involved removing an inch in diameter of skin and tissue from where the growth was, and graft a like amount from my rear end. He could tell I was hesitant about the whole situation. His eyes narrowed as he shot at me, "I don't think you realize how serious this is. The kind of melanoma you have is fatal if we don't catch it in time. If not arrested, it attacks various glands, specifically lymph nodes." I finally got the picture. I walked out of his office in a daze.

Susan had been waiting for me, and we walked out to the car. I told her the story. She reached over and put her hand on mine and said, "Don't worry, everything will be O.K." Those next few days were like living in a dream. I was withdrawing from my family, friends and associates, and could feel the distance grow. Such a lonely feeling when death is knocking. That was a strange and contemplative time for me.

Would this infirmity end my search forever? How valuable time becomes when it isn't as open-ended. I had wanted to know the mysteries of my past before the sand finished its inexorable run through life's hour glass. Now this cancer thing. Was this something I had inherited? Maybe my natural father or mother were already long dead from such a disorder. Why had I procrastinated so long in finding them? I might never know. If God pulled me through this hard time, I resolved to intensify my efforts in unlocking the door to my past.

The day before my surgery, my doctor called me at the office and said he had five other pathologists look at my growth specimen. They had a long consultation, and the major opinion was my growth was not malignant as originally diagnosed, but somewhere in-between. He had cancelled my surgery! Good news! I felt like shouting and dancing. Life for me quickly got back on track.

In the summer of 1975 our organization was merged with a larger one, The Army & Air Force Exchange Service, headquartered in Dallas, Texas. We sure hated to leave our friends and our home in Virginia. I was then transferred to Dallas, where I started my professional life all over again. Those were interesting times, as I made new friends and found my nitch anew.

For the next twelve years I would "search" as the mood struck. The urge would come about every four or five years, and would last two to three days. The four-to-five year cycle pretty much followed my company transfers. The search consisted of calling information assistance in various cities as I did in Virginia, and asking for a listing of Andrew or Rebecca Kullberg. I continued to call an occasional Kullberg, and ask if they knew of an Andrew or Rebecca. In March, 1976, after several cycles with zero results, I decided to write the Children's Home Society of California. They responded with general information, some of which I already knew. However, it gave good thumb nail sketches of my natural parents, as well as an insight into the reason for my adoption. It read in part:

Your biological mother was twenty-six years old at the time of your birth. She was of German and English descent and of the Protestant religion. She was a high school graduate and had attended business school. She is described as being 5'2" in height and weighed 145 lbs. The only physical description we have describes her as having a light complexion.

Your natural father was twenty-five years of age at the time of your birth. He was of Italian descent and of the Catholic religion.

He was a high school graduate and was self-employed as the owner of a liquor store. He is described as having dark eyes and dark hair, and being nice looking.

Your biological mother was a housewife at the time of your birth. She was married to another man when she met your father. She had two children with her husband. Because of the circumstances of your birth, your biological mother felt that she could not offer you the security and attention to which all children are entitled. Her husband, (Scandinavian and blonde) was upset by her relationship with your father, and he requested that a child of this relationship not live in his home. Therefore, your mother believed that in the best interest of all involved, she would arrange for your adoption.

61

Several new pieces of information surfaced. It was apparent by the physical description of my natural mother, that my propensity for gaining weight came from her. For a woman to attend a business school back in those days, she must have been bright and good with numbers. She picked a younger man to have an affair with, which seemed unusual. The thing that continued to baffle me was why it took eighteen months to start the adoption process. I focused on the phrase, "she could not offer you security." Especially with an irate husband and a dark reminder toddling around. An earlier letter from the Children's Home, saved in the box, indicated the staff was aware of my situation from birth. That same letter stated my availability for adoption as December 1942, eighteen months later. What happened during those eighteen months?

I must admit, when I first read the above letter, some of the ambition to find my natural parents was dampened. The realization of my untimely entrance into this world was distasteful. But, that's what life had dealt me. In other ways, I guess I was lucky; if this had happened to me twenty-five years later, I could well have been aborted. I have always had strong "right-to-life" feelings.

When I thought about the circumstances of my conception and birth, I thanked God my natural mother didn't do away with me. She must have been a good and brave person. If I ever found her, I made myself a promise to thank her for letting me grow in her body and giving birth to me. I will thank her for my three sons as well. She let us all have life—wonderful life.

I made several tries with outside assistance in my search activities. I wrote several adoptive search organizations, which included sending membership fees, but never heard from them. What a disappointment! I really had high hopes that one of them would come through with a computer match, as they had advertised. That was five years ago. In addition, I contacted a "Private Eye" in Los Angeles, who specialized in locating people. I had no success and began to doubt the existence of my natural parents.

This made the task seem impossible.

It was frustrating, but challenging. It was like playing an intriguing game of chess. However, I was running out of moves and it was starting to look like I would lose.

From the time my Dad gave me the box of letters, he has never asked me if I used the information to search for my natural parents. He hasn't mentioned anything close to the subject. However, over the years, my stepmother has asked me on several occasions if I have made any attempts to seek out my past. I denied any efforts and pretty much left the impression that I didn't feel the need. Since my search inclinations were few and far between, I didn't feel too guilty about my prevarication. I wondered why she was asking me. The only time I've come close to telling my Dad was when I asked him if he had ever regretted not having his own child. I couched the question by assuring him I would understand if his answer was affirmative. His response was immediate. I *was* his child as far as he was concerned! I never brought up the subject again.

We bought a place in Arlington, Texas, located midway between Dallas and Fort Worth. Northern Texas weather took getting used to, as it was hotter than hell in the summer, and icy cold in the winter. Texans are a friendly, outgoing lot, and we felt at home in no time. The boys adjusted well to their new lives.

To escape the hot Texas summers, we spent many vacations in the Colorado Rockies. Somehow, we always managed to work in a visit with Unc at Green Mountain Falls, and what super times we had! One summer we took Unc with us for a few days to Rocky Mountain National Park. He stayed back at our cabin, reading and babysitting our dog, Fred, while we hiked from one end of the park to the other.

In July 1979, I was transferred to our San Francisco Regional Office. I was going back to California, and that was cause for celebrating. It was good to be near Dad again, and we visited often. We lived in Concord, about twenty-five miles east of San Francisco. The commute was a long, tedious ordeal, that took an hour on good days. It was a year before I became accustomed to those early mornings that seemed more like middle-of-the-nights. Otherwise, it was great to be living in paradise again.

We never lacked for things to do. Sue and I loved San Francisco, and went in for dinner and a show whenever we could. The Carnelian Room on top of the Bank of America building was a favorite spot for cocktails. From there the view of the city and Bay was absolutely enchanting! Another favorite was going to a concert at the Concord Pavilion. There was nothing quite like relaxing on the lawn with friends, while drinking wine with a gourmet picnic supper, and listening to the New York Philharmonic or Count Basie play to the stars. Sweet memories! Vacations were a problem because it was difficult to decide where to go. My preference was Lake Tahoe or Yosemite, while Susan chose the coast.

My work took me all over the nine western states. I would occasionally look in phone directories or call information operators, but no Andrew or Rebecca Kullberg. There were several times I went to Los Angeles on business. On one occasion, I decided to visit the Children's Home Society of California at 3100 West Adams Boulevard. I wanted to see first-hand where I had emerged when I was eighteen months old. I planned to visit with one of the social workers, and attempt to elicit some new clues about myself.

When I arrived at 3100 West Adams, the Children's Home was not there anymore. I found their new address and paid them a visit. They were the most closed-mouth group of people I'd ever run across. They could sense I was an adoptee the moment I walked into the building. I approached the receptionist and asked to see a social worker, and she asked, "Adoptee?" I replied, "Yes." When I sat down to discuss my situation, I might as well have been talking to a brick wall. My Italian blood started to heat up, and I knew I'd best leave before I lost my temper. I felt like shouting, "I have the right to know who I am!" But I realized it wasn't the Home Society's doing. It was the law. I

64

often wondered why information couldn't be given if all parties mutually agreed. The Home Society could act as the agency for coordinating the agreements or lack thereof. I understand the rights and sensitivities of others involved in such a personal situation, and would never advocate information on demand. Consent by the principle parties is necessary.

All too soon, in January 1983, I was transferred back to Dallas. Since it was in the middle of the school year, I went by myself. That was the toughest move I ever had to make. To be without family for six months was a huge sacrifice. My family was aggravated and didn't want to leave California, but I had no choice. They joined me in June, and as usual, time heals all. We became happy Texans again.

My three sons have all done well. Even though the moves have been difficult for them at times, I think the varied experiences of life in different locations have been valuable. They have all done exceedingly well academically. David has graduated from UC Berkeley with a degree in Engineering Physics. John is studying Electrical Engineering at the University of Texas in Austin. Mike is a senior in high school, and has been accepted at Austin in the School of Engineering. I think I'll quit my job and manage the future Deatherage Engineering Firm!

Major outside interests of mine have been in tournament bridge and chess. Both are fantastic games. I have been playing chess more in recent years. I like to play in at least one national tournament and in three or four locals during the year. The wide variety of people who play tournament chess would make an excellent anthropology study. Several years back, I was playing in the World Open in Philadelphia. I wasn't having my best tournament. I had won four of seven games going into my last battle. Lo and behold, I was playing a young fellow eleven years old. He came over very gentlemanly, shook my hand, and we set up the pieces. The game started. Pretty soon there was a crowd around our game. It then dawned on me that this kid was probably nationally ranked. He was number eight in his age category. Things were going smoothly. The only part that bothered me was he'd move and then leave the table. I'd spend five minutes and move, and he'd literally run back and move instantly, and then leave again. I figured at my age, my brain circuits just weren't that fast anymore. I continued to take my time. The spectators would look at me and I sensed they were pulling for the "kid." Their looks said, "Why not let him win?" There were two adults that showed up more often than the others. They were the kid's parents. Anyway, the game continued and we were on about move eighteen, when the "kid" overlooked a devious attack move I had planned. This time I moved immediately, which took him off-guard. He settled down and studied the situation. He started to squirm a little. I knew he knew. He'd been had. He looked up and banged the table with a clenched fist, yelling, "God dammit!" I almost had a heart attack. I just didn't expect that. Chess games are usually rather quiet. There were over five-hundred people playing in the hall and everybody within twenty tables around us looked over our way. My opponent hadn't moved yet, so I got up and moved away. He was still cussing a blue streak, but more to himself. I came back in five minutes. He had moved. My moves were easy then, and didn't require alot of time, so I moved right off. After about three more moves, it was certain I was moving in on his king. He asked if I wanted a draw (tie). I looked at him and said, "You'd be disappointed if I accepted a draw." He just smiled and resigned.

In April 1986, I decided to try a different approach in my search. I located and contacted my old friend with the Social Security Administration. I asked if he would mind checking to see if there was a listing for Andrew or Rebecca Kullberg in California. It seemed like cheating, an illegal chess move, but I was at the end of my rope. He said he'd try.

At first he was reluctant. I think he was concerned that his people might discover he was conducting a private party search. That was forbidden. I had hoped he could search throughout the United States, but that was impossible. It had to be on a state-by-state basis. Initially, he had to find out what snags he would run into. Namely, what people or programs would have to be overcome. He didn't want a trail. He had no idea why I was interested in finding these people, other than they were old friends. That was one more responsibility I was shouldering. What if I found and aggravated the Kullbergs, and they demanded to know or found out how I contacted them? My friend would definitely be in a precarious position. I would not let that happen.

Three or four days went by without hearing from him. I figured another dead end, and had almost forgotten about it when he called. He had an address and a birthdate! I couldn't believe it! The name was Andrew Eugene Kullberg, born in 1938 and lived in Camarillo, California. If he was the right Kullberg, with that birthdate, he must be my half-brother. I asked my friend if he had any trouble and he replied, "No complications, everything was O.K." I thanked him and within five minutes was talking with the information operator in Camarillo.

My heart was pounding in anticipation as I asked for the phone number of Andrew Kullberg. There was a pause. The operator said there was no listing! How could that be! Fate was playing a trick on me. I asked the operator if she was sure. She said there was definitely no listing for an Andrew Eugene Kullberg. I think the operator probably sensed my disbelief and emotional tension, because she recommended that maybe the sheriff's office could help. She put me right through (no charge).

The Camarillo Sheriff's Office confirmed the nonexistence of a resident by the name of Andrew Kullberg. I had the presence of mind to ask if they would give me the phone number of the people living at the address my friend had given me. Without hesitation, they gave it to me and I called. A man answered and said he didn't know anybody by the name. Damn! He said that he had lived at this address for only a year, and didn't know the previous owner's name. I asked if he'd mind giving me one of the neighbor's phone numbers, and he obliged. In fact, he gave me both adjacent neighbors' phone numbers, as well as the people who lived across the street. I thanked him very much. At this point, I was getting rather discouraged. What looked like a sure thing was turning into a frustrating effort which led into brick walls.

I called the neighbor who lived across the street. A man answered. I asked if he had known the Kullbergs who lived across the street. He remembered them! What a relief. It renewed my faith in Social Security. My excitement index was at record level.

The "across the street" neighbor was friendly and accommodating. I introduced myself as a childhood friend of "Andy's," saying I hadn't seen him in thirty years. The neighbor said the Kullbergs had moved away three years ago. He remembered them as a close family. He said Andy had a wonderful wife, whom he married in Spain, and two sons, one in college. He worked for the Navy as some kind of civilian engineer. He said they had become homesick for the East Coast, after living in California for only one year, and moved back to either South or North Carolina.

When I heard about their being homesick for the East Coast, I felt a seed of doubt. The Andy Kullberg I was looking for was a native Californian. When I told him this, the neighbor said, "Oh yes, Andy was born and raised in Los Angeles. In fact, he has a sister who still lives in the L.A. area. It's just that Andy and his family have lived the past twenty years or so somewhere on the Southeast Coast." I asked him if he remembered Andy talking about his mother, and he said, "I don't think she ever visited him, but I recall Andy talking about her, and I think he said she lives somewhere in California." I thanked him for his help. I was sure that this Andrew E. Kullberg was my older half-brother, and it sounded as if my natural mother was still alive!

I called the South Carolina information operator and asked in the best Texas drawl I could muster, if she'd help me find an Andrew E. Kullberg who probably lived in a city near a navy base. Thank God there was only one area code for South Carolina. She was most helpful and patient. She checked out four or five metro areas, with no luck. I was about to thank her and move on to North Carolina when she said, "Let's try Beaufort," and there it was. Checkmate! It just wasn't possible for that operator to know how grateful I was for her assistance, even though I tried.

When I think about the odds of successfully tracking down that precious phone number, I realized that God, luck or fate, was with me. First off, I'm not sure, and never asked why Social Security still had Andrew Kullberg listed at a Camarillo address when he hadn't lived there in three years. Also, if my friend had come up empty in the California search, chances are good I wouldn't have pursued other states. Certainly, South Carolina would have been one of the last states, considering population alone. However, once I obtained that address, it didn't matter how long ago he had lived there or what the circumstances, I was determined to find my prize. I didn't care what it demanded and was ready to personally go to Camarillo and investigate.

Knowing I was a phone call away from the "other side" sent shivers up my spine, and put my mind to spinning. How would this journey affect me? My life would be changed forever. Was I capable of enduring the worst possible scenario, which might unfold? I tried to imagine what revelation could strike at my soul. I would be vulnerable to rejection, but could overcome that. If I found my past existence was the cause of alot of hurt, and lives were adversely altered, it would bother me, but I could bury that within. Hard facts like hereditary diseases, short life spans and mental illness would be tough to accept, but understood. If their values, morals or ethics were the antithesis of mine, I'd be disappointed, and would quickly close the door to my past. I soon realized I could deal with almost anything the "other side" could throw at me, save one. If Dad, or my family were hurt in any way, I wouldn't be able to forgive myself.

When I called, what should I say? What if he didn't know anything about me? Would my calling upend family relationships on the "other side"? Maybe it would be best if I didn't disturb the Kullbergs after all. Would my resurrection cause ill or good feelings? How would my Dad feel if he found out? Would it hurt him? God knows that's the last thing I'd want to happen. I couldn't know where or when the reactions would end or how lives would be altered. I spent three days agonizing over such issues. In the end, I decided in favor of truth, but promised myself to back off if there was resistance or reluctance on the "other side."

I decided to call midday, when "Andy" would be working. I'd talk with his wife and get a general feel of things like family sensitivities. I'd keep it low-keyed and simple. That seemed like a good, passive plan. No initial confrontations, information-gathering only. I was ready to make my phone call.

The Other Side

On April 29, 1986, I made the usual commute to my Dallas office. It was like any other except this day I would reach out across time in an attempt to touch my past . . . to unlock the secrets of my existence. The long distance phone call to Beaufort, South Carolina would truly be distant, as though to another dimension. I wondered if Mom had considered the possibilities when she wrote the names Andrew and Rebecca Kullberg on the envelope preserved in the box. Could she have imagined that one day her son would use the disclosure to reunite with his flesh and blood? I wanted to believe she would understand my relentless pursuit. My peace of mind and spirit depended on it.

I had spent a restless and sleepless night rehearsing the anticipated conversation with Andrew Kullberg's wife, Angela, while trying to foresee the consequences. Prepared notes and a form designed to record my historic moment were ready for use. I realized there was a good chance no one would be home at that time of day, but decided to stick with my passive plan. There was a part of me that would feel relief if the "rings" went unanswered.

At about eleven-thirty in the morning, Central Standard Time, I connected with the long-distance operator to charge the call to my home phone number. The operator said, "Thank you for using AT&T, have a nice day," and the phone started ringing at the Andrew Eugene Kullberg residence in Beaufort, South Carolina. It rang and rang. Just as I was beginning to think no one was going to answer, someone picked up the phone. From the time I heard the consummating "click," until the expected feminine voice responded, it seemed an eternity.

Finally, the solitary word came. "Hello."

To my consternation, a mature male voice answered. For an instant I almost hung up. It took every ounce of strength I had to ask, "Is this the Andrew Kullberg residence?"

"Yes," he replied, "this is Andy Kullberg."

My scheme had collapsed. It was time to wing it. After a short pause to regroup my thoughts, I forced out, "My name is Gary Deatherage."

"Yes?" he inquired.

My tense state made breathing difficult. Gulping for air, I continued, "I think we knew each other some forty-four years ago. . . in Los Angeles. I was. . ."

He broke in before I could mutter another word and asked, "Are you my brother, Gary?"

I was dumfounded. I couldn't believe what I had heard. Almost immediate recognition! It was as though he was expecting a call from me. After clearing my throat, I said, "Yes, I think I am."

"I'll be damned!" he retorted. "Where are you calling from. . . where have you been all these years?"

"I'm living in the Dallas, Texas area now," I replied, "but have moved a half-dozen times or so over the past twenty years."

Andy said, "I just can't believe it; I don't know where to begin; tell me all about yourself." In the background I could hear him telling Angela, "This is Gary, the brother I told you about."

I began, "I was born June 3, 1941, in Los Angeles, and left your home sometime in November, 1942. . ."

Andy interrupted, "Yes, that's right. I remember your birthdate, as mine is June 13th." He paused and in a more somber tone, said, "And I remember when you left us." He exclaimed, "This is just fantastic! Tell me this is really happening. . . ."

We continued on for a half-hour or so. It was the beginning of a bizarre, dreamlike time for me. Events and information came fast, almost too fast to assimilate. My life has usually been at a slow, deliberate, thought-out, easy-going pace. Some of the things I was to learn about myself were nothing short of amazing.

Andy later told me that he knew it was me, his brother, the second I gave my name, Gary. He said it was a strange feeling—like ESP. Andy was very young when I was at their home, and didn't remember much. But he said there was a scene, which was projected in his mind while I talked to him that first time. We were taking a bath together. I had decided to eat the bar of soap. Andy said he just sat and watched me and giggled. Our mother came into the bathroom and gave him hell for letting me chew on soap.

Andy and I had an amiable long chat. He is outgoing, personable, and candid. After he discovered I was his "long, lost brother" he said, "Well, thank God you're not Fabian or Elvis Presley!" It seems his mother thought at one point that I had turned out to be Fabian, and more recently, Elvis Presley. I assured him that it was all I could do to carry a tune and fame had not touched me. Before we went too far into our conversation, I told Andy I didn't want to barge into his life if it was going to be a burden—that if he had any reservations, I'd simply hang up and he wouldn't hear from me again. Andy said, "Are you kidding? Don't you dare hang up!" My resurrection was good and exciting news.

Andy Kullberg was born June 13, 1938 in Los Angeles, California. He attended elementary school near their Berkeley Avenue home, and went to several high schools, graduating from Manhatten Beach High School in 1956. After obtaining an Associate's Degree at Barstow Junior College, he went into the Air Force. He had a tour in Spain and grew to love the people and their culture, becoming fluent in Spanish. He met Angela, fell in love, and eventually married her. Andy's family back home was less than enthusiastic about his marriage to a Spanish girl, and he had a difficult time getting the consent necessary for a Catholic wedding. They have two sons, and are a loving, close-knit family.

Andy asked if I had brothers and sisters, and when I

told him no, he said, "Well, you do now!" I found out that I have six half-brothers and sisters all over the country. He said his older sister, ReeAnn, who lives in California, would be anxious to hear about me. They had often wondered what fate had befallen me after I left their home on Berkeley Avenue in Los Angeles. Andy said ReeAnn would be able to give me more details about that time in my life. She was several years older and had an excellent memory of those days. I asked him where our mother, Rebecca, was living, and he said he didn't know. He hadn't seen her in fifteen years, and rarely talked with her, only when she called him. He said his life with his mother had been painful and he really didn't want to communicate with her now.

Andy's insistence that he didn't know where Rebecca was or how to contact her led me to believe he was trying to shield her from me, which I understood and appreciated. I figured he wanted to make sure about me before allowing access. I would be just as cautious. At times, however, his technique for putting me off was rather curious. Andy asked, "Even if I knew how to reach Rebecca, are you sure you really want to contact her?" I didn't know how to answer that rhetorical question. Why wouldn't I want to communicate with my natural mother? He continued, "If you contact her, it's a two-edged sword, as she'll know where you are." His approach of derailing my desire to find her was shrewd and effective. Andy had delivered his veiled warning so skillfully that I had no idea what to think. I felt something in the pit of my stomach, perhaps the slightest sting of fear. I didn't know how to solve the riddle. Andy gave no specifics and I didn't press, as there was plenty of time. I'd wait and let the Kullbergs tell me when and where to seek Rebecca. After all, there were five other siblings to check in with. I asked him if he knew my natural father's name. He didn't. He just knew that he was Italian and owned a neighborhood liquor store.

Out of the clear blue, Andy asked, "How'd you find me?" For some reason I wasn't prepared to answer, and fumbled a bit. I explained about the box of letters and my mom's handwritten note, showing the names, Andrew and Rebecca Kullberg. Everything went fine to that point. Then, instead of mentioning the Social Security connection, I lied. I told him a friend who lives in Camarillo mentioned that an Andrew Kullberg had lived there in recent years. I continued with the events as they actually happened. Andy asked which neighbor I talked with, and I said the one who lived across the street. He seemed satisfied with my explanation. I hadn't thought of rehearsing my story. The part about my hypothetical friend was weak, but the best I could extemporaneously muster. I was afraid Andy would ask who my friend was and how he knew his address. That reply would have been weaker.

Andy gave me the names and what he knew of my half-sisters and brother. ReeAnn was living in the Los Angeles area. She had four children by her first marriage, and is now living with her second husband. By the way he talked, Andy is closest to ReeAnn and Hallie. Hallie lives close to Andy in the Beaufort area, and is living by herself now. She has four children. Hallie was born right after I left in November 1942. Jean lives in Phoenix, Arizona, and was brought up by her Aunt Sarah Ellen and Uncle Woody. They adopted her. Sarah Ellen is Rebecca's next younger sister. Jean, Hallie, Andy and ReeAnn all had the same natural father, Andrew Kullberg, Sr. Kathleen was born after Hallie, and Andy didn't really know much about her. He didn't know where she lived or anything about her adult life. George, the youngest, was living in Texas, or so he thought. Andy had talked with him on the phone when George was a teenager, but not since. Evidently, it was a rather heated discussion about their mother, and they parted under less than cordial conditions. He knew George had become a ward of the State of Texas, and had had several foster parents. Like me, Kathleen and George were the products of different fathers. It was evident and understandable that the Kullberg children were close, whereas George and Kathleen were outsiders. I wasn't sure where I fit in. As we talked, and he was trying to recall various family facts, I could hear Angela, his wife, helping with the family history. Very much like it would be if someone called me, wanting to know family background. Sue would be needed. Andy didn't ask much about my adopted family, and what he did ask, I gave unidentifiable information. When he asked, "What happened to you after leaving our Berkeley Avenue house in Los Angeles? Where did you live?" I was vague. Mentioning that I had attended school in Oregon and lived in Texas for many years, helped disguise the fact that my home was only sixty miles away from Los Angeles. I was extremely sensitive to the possibility of one of the Kullbergs ever tracking down and contacting Dad.

That was the extent of the information passed on during that first call in late April. We ended the conversation promising to keep in touch and visit each other at the earliest chance.

For at least fifteen minutes after the call, I sat in my office with the doors still shut. The elation I was experiencing was euphoric. I was in a dimension that was light years away from the reality of my office confines. I got up and walked around, and it was like I was floating. The tension had built up inside me. Suddenly, as though it were an involuntary reaction, I cried out, "I found them! Thank you God!" Those words bounced around my office walls and tears welled up in my eyes. In a minute or two I composed myself and opened my office doors. When I walked out, I realized my life would never be the same.

The first contact with the "other side" was truly a remarkable and memorable encounter. The sky didn't fall, and indeed, my worst fears were put to rest—at least for now. My brother Andy seemed genuinely happy to know me as his brother again.

I had called during lunch time and my mind was miles away from work concerns the rest of the afternoon. I hadn't told anybody of my personal discovery, except Susan, and my insides were bursting until I could get home and tell her of the conversation with my brother.

When I came home from work that day, I rushed in the

76

house to tell Sue my news. Several days before I had told her that I thought I had my brother's phone number. She had no idea that I was calling that day, let alone at noon. I didn't tell her because I didn't want to be tied down to a set time. It had to be when I was ready to call. Now that was all history.

I finally found Susan working in the yard. I came up to her and asked, "Guess who I talked with today?" After a short pause, I said, "My brother, Andy Kullberg." Her surprised look had a touch of disbelief.

Then the name you found was really him," she remarked.

"Yes, he was the one," I said.

I believe I saw a few tears in her eyes. She could tell my anxiety level was off the end of the scale. She looked at me and asked, "Are you alright?" I assured her I was okay.

Waiting for the repercussions was nerve-racking. At this point, God only knew who was talking to whom, and what was being said on "the other side". Now a new worry was beginning to grip me. I was already feeling guilty about my Dad and how he'd react if he ever found out. My God, what had I done? There would be several more sleepless nights, as there were before I called.

Sue calmed me down. She told me that time would take care of things—that this was meant to be. I don't think I could have kept my sanity without her help.

I told her what Andy had told me about my siblings, and the general state of affairs when I lived with the Kullbergs. When I asked Andy what he remembered of my short life with them, his demeanor seemed to take on a more serious note. The lighthearted quality of his earlier voice dropped an octave and the previously easy flow of words slowed to a more guarded pace. It was clear that life during my tenure at his home was anything but pleasant. Andy said his father was "upset" with my presence, and was constantly trying to get his mother to give me up for adoption. When I started to follow up for particulars, he begged off, saying ReeAnn would be able to give a more complete picture. I got the impression I was prying into a part of Andy's childhood which he didn't want to remember, or if he did, he was reluctant to pass it on to me. So, I dropped it.

The strange thing was that Andy didn't know where his mother was or hadn't seen her in many years. That was unreal to me. In my family that could never happen. The only explanation was that he was protecting her from me. Sue agreed.

It was all I could do to keep my wits about me that evening during dinner. My usually ravenous appetite was nonexistent, and it was all Sue could do to keep me calmed down as I paced around the house. What next? That question was soon answered. At approximately nine o'clock that night our phone rang. It was ReeAnn, my older sister calling from California. Sue answered the phone, and after a short conversation, she called me over, saying, "It's ReeAnn from Los Angeles."

When I took the phone, the person on the other end said, "Hi Gary, this is your sister, ReeAnn. We have lots to talk about, don't we?"

"We sure do," I said, "but please be patient with me. Today has been a big day in my life."

"I know what you mean," she said, "I was just telling your wife it must be something to have a husband who brings home stray brothers and sisters."

I said, "ReeAnn, when I think back on my phone call with your. . . I mean our brother, Andy, it's amazing. I'm still numb and not sure this hasn't been a dream."

"I know," she said.

ReeAnn is a very pleasant person to talk with. She would have been a great older sister even if she was bossy, like Andy says. I felt right at home with her in the first several minutes. Her speech is slow and deliberate, like mine, and has a joy to it that puts one at ease. She began by welcoming me to the family. She told me that when Andy called her earlier to pass on the good news of my existence, she wept tears of happiness. It made me feel good to hear her say that. She wanted to know if Andy had characterized her as the "bossy one" when they were little. I denied it and told her he had nothing but good things to say. One of the first questions she asked me was whether I had a good sense of humor, as though it was going to be necessary as my young life unraveled.

Everything considered, she and Andy had a fairly happy childhood. She told me several stories about her life when they lived at the Berkeley Avenue house. ReeAnn fondly recalled that she and Andy entertained the kids on the block by singing and dancing. They were both musically inclined. They charged admission and made enough for ice cream. She and Andy would go down to my natural father's place, since he sold ice cream as well as liquor. I asked if she knew his name, and she thought it was Frank, but didn't know his last name. We casually traded stories for fifteen minutes or so, and then came a bolt of lightning. She proceeded to literally blow my mind!

ReeAnn asked me if I knew that I had been adopted right after birth. I told her no, that I was adopted when I was eighteen months old. She seemed surprised that I didn't know about my first adoption. After a slight pause, as if debating whether to go on, my sister, very matter-of-factly said, "Gary, you'll find this hard to believe, but you were adopted by Joan Crawford when you were about ten days old."

I retorted, "You're kidding me!" This was incredulous. Was this some kind of trick my family from the "other side" had concocted?

She said, "It's very much the truth, and I think you'll find your story fascinating."

I asked, "Did you say Joan Crawford, the actress, was my adopted mother at birth?"

She replied, "Yes! Have you ever read *Mommie Dearest* by Christina Crawford?"

I replied, "Not for a long time."

ReeAnn said, "Well, there's a part in the book about you where Joan Crawford had to return her second adopted child, who was you, because his natural mother found out where he was and demanded his return." All this was blowing my mental circuits, but ReeAnn proceeded to tell me the incredible story.

ReeAnn remembered Andy and herself tagging along on several occasions when her mom was on a date with Frank, my natural father. She tells of him being dark and good looking, and always having alot of candy for them. ReeAnn said most of their dates were at other family liquor stores. I asked, "How many stores were there?"

She replied, "Five or six."

ReeAnn iterated she could understand her mother's attraction to Frank, a very handsome man.

ReeAnn vividly recalled a particular outing. The four of them, Rebecca, Frank, Andy and ReeAnn, went for an afternoon ride in the country near Los Angeles, up and down dirt roads, and through and around orange tree orchards. Finally they stopped. My father gave ReeAnn and Andy a box of candy, and told them to go for a walk. They hiked off and the candy was eaten. She and Andy came back earlier than the amorous couple expected. There was a flurry of activity as clothes flew and zippers zipped. ReeAnn mused that she probably witnessed my conception. The result, of course, was that Rebecca was soon pregnant with me, her third child.

Along about the seventh month, Rebecca felt guilty and confessed to her husband that she wasn't carrying his child. ReeAnn says that's when severe times came to their home. Her Dad was filled with rage and threatened physical harm. He was a big, strong Swede (blonde) and a butcher by trade. Her mother feared for our safety, and reluctantly decided to put me up for adoption right after birth with a private "baby broker," Alice Hough.

The broker arranged for hospital expenses, child care of older children, plus some monetary compensation. Alice Hough happened to deal with Hollywood stars. ReeAnn said she and Andy stayed with Penny Singleton, (of "Blondie" fame), for a short while when it was close to my delivery time.

I have since talked with Penny Singleton, who sounds just like she did thirty years ago in her show, "Dagwood and Blondie". I really enjoyed talking with her. She remembered Andy and ReeAnn very well, and loved having them stay with her. She said that back in those days, she occasionally took temporary care of children for Alice Hough.

She recalled that Rebecca came and visited, and was very much pregnant with me, so much so that Penny was concerned she might "drop" me right there on the spot. Penny remembered hearing about my natural father being Italian and owning some kind of store.

Penny wanted to know more about ReeAnn and Andy, and I told her what I knew. I told her I'd given ReeAnn her phone number. Over the years she had hoped ReeAnn and Andy would look her up.

Even though our conversation was amiable enough, Penny seemed reticent when we talked, as if she was afraid of my connection with her past. At the time, I was interested in getting a line on Alice Hough, hoping that she was still alive, so I could contact her. Penny said she would try to find out what happened to Hough. Later I learned she died. Her relationship with Alice Hough appears to have been close, from her own account, as well as ReeAnn's chronicles. She may have personal reasons for not wanting to open that chapter again.

I have talked to her several times, and on one occasion gave her some of my background. Knowing that she lived somewhere in the San Fernando Valley vicinity, I mentioned having attended Harvard Military. She said, "Oh yes, I'm familiar with the school. My husband and I helped fund the construction of the chapel many years ago."

ReeAnn tells me that living with Penny Singleton was truly a magical experience. Penny was like a fairy godmother to her and Andy. She was loving, gentle and always happy. ReeAnn says Andy was asked by a social worker where he wanted to live as it came time to go home. He didn't hesitate to say at Aunt Penn's. It took the social worker some time to convince Andy he should return to his mother and father. Penny mentioned that she had asked Rebecca early on if it might be possible to keep Andy and ReeAnn. Rebecca had indicated maybe, raising Penny's hopes. After I was born, Penny asked Alice Hough about keeping Andy and ReeAnn. The answer was no. Penny told me she and her husband couldn't bare to be present when Andy and ReeAnn's parents came for them, so they left the house that day.

I was born on June 3, 1941. Rebecca and I stayed in the hospital approximately nine days. When it came time to leave the hospital, Andrew Kullberg and Alice Hough helped Rebecca, with me in her arms, to Hough's car. It was early afternoon. Now was the time for separating mother from child. Rebecca was having second thoughts and didn't want to give me up. Hough and Kullberg, Sr. had joined forces. Alice Hough reasoned with Rebecca, "You already have two delightful children, ReeAnn and Andy. Why take this little Italian baby home and spoil everything?" Of course, Kullberg was in full agreement. Rebecca's resistance was fading. Rebecca complained that her friends and neighbors would see her come home without her baby. Alice Hough was ready for that one. Rebecca and her new son would go to Alice's home and later that night, or early the next morning, Hough would take Rebecca home. Alice Hough dropped Kullberg off at his home, and took Rebecca and me home with her.

It was a fine palatial residence. Rebecca was not accustomed to such elegance. It was evident Hough was handsomely rewarded for her craft.

Rebecca was escorted to an upstairs bedroom where she was to rest until nightfall. I had been taken to a nursery, somewhere on the first floor. Night came and Rebecca was starting to get restless. She didn't feel like resting anymore. It had been five or six hours since our arrival. Then she heard a car pull up outside. A limousine like she had never seen before was idling in the circular drive down below the bedroom window. It was a Duesenberg. Then she saw two women rush out to the car, and one was carrying something. It was a babe in a blanket. It was Rebecca's baby—me! Alice Hough took Rebecca home later that night.

After a short time, things settled down at the Kullberg residence. Andy and ReeAnn returned home after living with Penny Singleton. Life was back to normal, or as much as it could be.

After several months, Rebecca started to feel guilty about giving up her child, and decided to pursue my return. Somehow, she found out that Joan Crawford had me. Rebecca claims that God told her where I was, but other accounts say there was a news release giving the exact birthdate, which led her to Crawford. She wrote letters to Alice Hough and Joan Crawford, demanding my return, threatening suit and negative publicity. Rebecca was successful, and I was returned to the Kullberg home in November of 1941.

Joan Crawford and Alice Hough returned me to the Berkeley Avenue house. Joan had on a pants suit, which made her appear to my young half-sister to be the husband of a bereaved couple, giving up their child. They carried me inside, and handed me over to Rebecca. Rebecca was sitting in an overstuffed chair with Andy on one arm and ReeAnn on the other. Rebecca proceeded to undress me, with ReeAnn and Andy observing closely, presumably to make sure I was not damaged merchandise. Alice Hough was furious and demanded that Rebecca stop such antagonistic antics while all the time Joan Crawford was crying and shouting obscenities at Rebecca. All too soon, Crawford and Hough left, leaving me behind. If they had known the hellish life I was condemned to for the next year, there would have been horror in their eyes.

The major part of the above account was related to me by ReeAnn.

Subsequent bits and pieces came from other siblings and relatives. ReeAnn's memory from childhood is remarkable, and I have verified most of her recollections by other sources. I must say, when she told me about being present at my probable conception, I was somewhat irritated. I remember thinking, "She's got her nerve." Later she apologized for being so blunt, but by then I had grown to appreciate her candor. All through the story, ReeAnn would point out reasons why her mom and dad did the things they did. ReeAnn told me she has thought about their lives for many years and has concluded they were all pawns of fate. I understood what she meant, the more my story unfolded.

Corroboration

After hearing this account of my early history, I contacted the *Los Angeles Times, Examiner,* and the National Film
Information Service to see if there were substantiating
news accounts. The information available was surprising. I
had no trouble obtaining articles, which verified this unbelievable story.

It was all there from several June 13, 1941 media
releases, telling of Joan Crawford's second child, baby
Christopher, to a later article by Louella Parsons, "Joan
Crawford's Loss of Adopted Son Real Heart Crushing
Story".

When I called the *Los Angles Times* Library, a young
lady answered. I asked her if she would send me any and
all articles about Joan Crawford and the adoption of her
children, from 1941 through 1942. She said it would be
difficult, since their information was indexed by date,
rather than subject matter. We started talking. I decided it
wouldn't hurt to tell her the reason for my request. When
she heard of the possibility that I once was adopted by
Joan Crawford, her interest level jumped ten-fold. She said
she'd dig out everything available on the subject. A week
later I received a thick envelope from the Los Angeles
Times. Inside were articles from June 1941 through April
1958. There were five or six that directly involved me or
Rebecca Kullberg through 1945. The others pertained to
Joan Crawford's second Christopher, and his various
attempts to run away. After reading those "runaway" articles, I remembered Christina Crawford's *Mommie Dearest*
and pulled it out to read again. Enclosed with the articles
was a nice note from the young lady who assisted me, say-

ing she hoped these articles would help, and wishing me luck. A week later I received newspaper clips from the National Film Information Service.

When I read the articles heralding Joan Crawford's adoption of a second child, I was puzzled. I focused in on the stated age of the new baby. The *Los Angeles Times* reported: "This time the infant is a boy, whom she has christened Christopher, and who is two months of age." The *Los Angeles Examiner* stated: "Adoption by Joan Crawford, MGM film star, of a five month old boy, whom she named Christopher, was announced yesterday by the studio". How could the two articles vary the age by so much? I realized, if it was me, it should read ten days old. Three other articles all gave different ages. I found out later that the press releases deliberately gave misleading ages or birthdates, so that the natural parents would not be able to trace who their child's adoptive parents were. Other first-hand accounts indicated the baby was newborn and only days old. I read several books about Joan Crawford, including: *Mommie Dearest, Joan Crawford: A Biography,* and *The Autobiography of Joan Crawford.* Most had references to the first baby Christopher.

Reading *The Autobiography of Joan Crawford* erased any doubts I had. Joan Crawford discussed the problems she had with her children's adoptions in Chapter Eight. She talks about the little boy she lost, not through death, but back to his original mother. Joan Crawford wrote:

The mother had given up the child when he was ten days old, but she'd changed her mind when she read in a published interview where he was. I'd made the mistake of mentioning his birthdate and birthplace. From that moment I had no peace. Day after day, she'd show up at my door. She sent threatening letters, demanding money. The situation assumed the aspects of a nightmare. My small son was entitled to life; I could not allow his being used as a pawn in the

*tug-of-war. So, I gave him back to the mother who
really didn't want him. Eventually the adoption home
stepped in, placing him where he couldn't possibly be
found.*

Until I read Joan Crawford's autobiography, I didn't
have any hard evidence of the baby's age at adoption. The
other books were vague on the point, and newspaper
accounts were unreliable. I searched high and low for the
published interview that purportedly mentioned my birthdate and birthplace, but never found it. Maybe it was in a
periodical that has long since gone out of circulation. Crawford's account makes it sound like Rebecca was trying to
extort money from her, and Crawford called her bluff. Joan
Crawford wasn't going to be coerced by anybody.

The *Los Angeles Examiner's* article by Louella Parsons
read in part:

> *The parting of Joan Crawford and her little son
> Christopher is one of Hollywood's most heart–break-
> ing stories. She had to stand by and see the little
> boy, used to every comfort and loving care and affec-
> tion, literally torn from her arms.*
>
> *She was powerless to do anything, even though
> the influential MGM Studio, moved by her grief, tried
> to see that she was permitted to keep the little boy
> who has learned to love her and whom Joan adored.*
>
> *There is much in the story that cannot be told. Joan,
> who loves little children, and found such happiness
> in her little adopted Christina, took baby Christopher
> when he was very tiny. She put him to bed every
> night, taught him to smile and laugh, and was happy
> when the doctors pronounced him a perfect baby.
> Then came the blow. The baby's parents, who had
> handed him over for adoption, learned that the adopt-
> ed mother was Joan Crawford.*
>
> *They decided they wanted him themselves and so
> Joan returned him. It was a blow to lose Christopher,*

who had become so dear to her and to take him
away from four–year old Christina, the beautiful little
blonde, blue-eyed daughter.

Louella Parsons gave me the first glimpse of myself as
Joan Crawford's son. Her article was the only one I found
which acknowledged that Crawford had lost her first son
back to his parents. The part that caught my eye was
where she said, *"there's much in the story that can't be
told,"* I understood what she meant the more my story
unfolded. Parsons' flowery rendition of the event is rather
stilted, but that probably was the style forty-six years ago. I
found out where I learned to smile and laugh, and that
doctors pronounced me a perfect baby.

Parson's article continued:

> *For the most part, Hollywood adoptions have been
> tremendously successful. Sandra and Ronnie Burns
> (Gracie Allen and George Burns' adopted youngsters)
> live up the street from me and if any two children
> have been showered with more advantages and love,
> I have never seen them.*
>
> *Joan Benny is the apple of Jack's eye and the Pat
> O'Briens spend hours talking about their three, and
> Bob and Delores Hope are crazy about Linda and
> Sonny, the Hopes' two adopted youngsters.*

Adoptions by Hollywood stars seemed to be in vogue
back in the early 1940's. In another part of the article, Parsons mentions that another Hollywood adoption met the
same fate as mine. She says Ann Southern brought home a
small boy, given to her by his parents. She was about to
adopt him and then the parents changed their minds, and
wanted him back. As Parsons put it, "There was nothing to
do, but return him, where he is one of many children."

Another segment of her lengthy article discussed Joan
Crawford's decision to return me. It read:

Baby Return Advisable—Joan couldn't bear to be without her baby's smiles and laughter. But wiser heads pointed out that it was advisable to return the baby. "How are you to know the child's family won't continue to ask for the baby if you don't give him up and then each year it will be harder to part with him . . ." her lawyer advised. So, Joan took him back to what, she doesn't know.

Hollywood stars who have adopted children and have obtained them through the Cradle, Mrs. Edna Gladney or any church orphanage, have nothing to worry about. No organization of this type would dream of telling the real parents the names of the adopted parents.

That's always a part of the bargain.

Such *bargains* are not the case in this day and age. The times of "closed adoptions" are rapidly becoming a thing of the past. Increasingly, adoption parents are being forced to agree to an "openness" atmosphere, where communication and contact between all parties is the rule.

I wrote Christina Crawford and asked if she would give me any information on the first baby Christopher. Making contact with Christina was one of my toughest challenges. It seems I spent weeks on finding a way to reach her. I had called her publisher, and sent a letter to her in care of same. I knew her married name, but was never able to get a lead. She had been involved with several public organizations, but no one knew or would tell me how to get in touch with her. I spent a fortune on phone calls alone. After several letters, I finally had a rewarding day at the mailbox. Her good letter arrived.

Christina's letter began by congratulating me on being so enterprising as to have retrieved so much information about my early past. She remembered Rebecca's rather wild visit to her home, and that there was a tremendous amount of yelling and screaming, shouting and swearing. Everyone in the house was scared to death. She knew that

Joan Crawford had given up the first baby Christopher. Christina says the problem arose when a newspaper interview listed the correct birthdate of the boy, leading the mother to connect him with Joan Crawford.

Christina gave some insight into the problems Joan had with the adoptions. Her letter read in part:

> *Because she was declared ineligible by the government adoption agency, she went through private means to acquire babies. My understanding is that she purchased all children and they went through a baby broker named Alice Hough. Mrs. Hough arranged the location and transfer of all details about the babies for her. I know that is true for the boy who came after the first one, and that is true for the two girls who arrived last.*
>
> *My understanding is that the first boy was never actually adopted. Crawford had a difficult time adopting any of us.*

She gave me several names of people who knew her mother well during this period and might be able to give me more details. One was a lady who was Joan Crawford's good friend and personal secretary of thirty years, Betty Barker. The other was Caesar Romero, the actor, who was a very close friend during that time.

When I first telephoned Betty Barker, she was reserved and guarded, and rightly so. Who would believe a wild story such as mine? She had me describe myself and give as much about dates and details as possible. She became convinced I was the Christopher Joan had given up. Joan's first Christopher had been dark complected with blue eyes and dark hair. He was in contrast with all the others she had adopted, who were fair-skinned and blonde.

Betty sent me a small print of the one and only picture of myself and Joan Crawford, which I had enlarged. By the looks of the baby, I was two months old at the time of the photo. Betty told me Joan often wondered what had happened to me up until the last years of her life. Betty Barker's letter to me read in part:

I think there is no doubt that you were Joan's first Christopher. She adored you and she was broken-hearted when she had to return you to your natural mother. I remember she wanted to fight the case, but her lawyers convinced her that she couldn't win. She destroyed all pictures of you except this one. Not for any personal reason against you, but just because seeing pictures of you brought back unhappy memories of losing you. She would have torn up this picture too, except that it was in a little sterling silver case to be carried in her purse, and she forgot she had it.

She always wondered what happened to you. I used to say, "You'll hear from him sometime," and she'd say, "I hope so." She would be so proud of you if only she knew.

I used to go on Joan's movie sets every Saturday (actors worked on Saturdays then), and she often had the nurse bring you on the sets with Christina in the late afternoons after your naps. Christina was trained to introduce you to everyone as , "This is my little brother Christopher." But we only saw you for about five or six months, then Joan lost you. I also saw you at her home several times. I remember you as being adorable with dark brown or black hair. (Christina had very blonde hair and coloring). You were chubby and a dream—absolutely the picture of health. I can't remember that you ever cried. She adored you as you were a perfect baby in every way. When she lost you, all of us were afraid to mention your name to her for years, as it was a tender subject with her. She would have loved to have known what happened to you. She did mention about your natural mother going to her door and trying to take you away, but that was long before I was her secretary.

She always used to say, "I had five children, but had to return one to his natural mother." She always seemed to feel that you were hers too.

I must have read Betty's letter a hundred times. There's something magical about seeing yourself as a baby, and Betty provided that for me, both in picture and description. Until then, my life began as an eighteen month old child. The photograph was black and white, and showed Joan Crawford holding me with my head resting on her shoulder and my hand holding her arm. Joan's head was canted toward mine, and she had a maternal smile, with a distant look in her eyes. The picture was taken looking straight at me with the left profile of my mother in the background. The look on my face reflected both contentment and contemplation.

I was returned to my natural mother in late November 1941. Thank God I can't remember the year that was to follow. From what I can tell, life must have been near hell for me. ReeAnn remembered my homecoming. She was happy at first to have her little baby brother back, whom she had never seen. Rebecca had ReeAnn hide me in the closet when her husband came home. It was supposed to be a secret that I was back. He soon found out, and ReeAnn tells me I was nothing more than a despised piece of meat. Unfortunately, I was a constant reminder of his wife's infidelity. When I cried at night, her father would become a mad man. Any reference to my existence created a rage. It was all Rebecca could do to prevent physical abuse to herself and me.

ReeAnn said her father would drink heavily after coming home from work. When he saw or heard me, he quickly transformed from a peaceful, loving person to a monster bent on destruction—my destruction! In my defense, Rebecca had to literally beat him off, and on several occasions grabbed the kitchen butcher knife, and went after him. To complicate matters, Rebecca became pregnant with her fourth child, fathered by Andrew Kullberg.

Even though I was only six months old, what a shock that must have been to be shuffled from a pampered, caring existence with Crawford, to a life where my survival was a day-to-day ordeal. When ReeAnn described the hateful atmosphere and deeds, I couldn't help but focus on my innocent vulnerability as a baby, and wondered what other despicable acts were committed. I quickly developed a hatred for a man I never knew, who was long dead. ReeAnn did her best to explain her father's plight, for the benefit of my understanding, but I must confess my feelings would not mend. In the end, there is never a good rational reason for abusing a child.

ReeAnn told me in a quiet, lamenting voice about meal times in their home. She seemed hesitant at first, and had a hard time getting started. ReeAnn said, "Gary, you weren't allowed to eat any meals with us. My father didn't want you near us. He wanted you out of the house! So my mother had no choice, but put you in a playpen on our front porch."

I was silent and let her continue. . . .

"You were not permitted to eat until after we had finished . . . you would peer in through the window while we ate . . . you were hungry, and you could see us eating at the table. We could hear you crying . . . and sobbing. We saw your tear–stained cheeks. Your sad face made us all feel so bad, except my father."

I didn't know what to say. . . .

She continued, "Gary, can you ever forgive us such torment? I have remembered your sad face all these years."

After about a year of cruel existence, at last Andrew Kullberg, Sr. almost did me in. He threw me across a room, and it ruptured my hernia! Rebecca rushed me to the hospital and made arrangements to give me up forever. My young Hell had ended. Several days later she gave birth to my half–sister, Hallie Marie.

That was in November 1942. On January 1, 1943, God brought my mom and dad to the Children's Home, and I went home with them. What a lucky day that was for us.

For many years we celebrated New Year's Day also as "Family Day." I'm not sure whether my Mom and Dad were ever aware of the sordid details of my young life. They never mentioned it.

I recently asked my Dad what he knew about my situation before he adopted me. He knew about the general backgrounds of my natural mother and father, and that my mother's husband wanted me out of his home. I asked if that was true, where was I from birth to eighteen months of age? He thought a second and said, "I guess you were at the Children's Home Society." Obviously, my parents didn't know much about my prior life.

In July 1986, I talked with a social worker at the Children's Home to see if there was any mention of my first adoption. She had pulled my file, and admitted that I had been adopted at birth, but didn't want to give me specific details. The California State Law would not permit disclosure of identifying information. She did say after looking at my file, that I would be a lot happier not knowing its contents. She said, "You really don't want to hear about this." Her voice was one of disbelief. My life had been a "real mess." However, just as we were about to end our conversation, she said, "Wait, here are several newspaper clippings on Joan Crawford's adoptions, and an article about a lady who forced her way into the Crawford residence." When I heard that, it was checkmate! I now had confirmation from the Children's Home Society of California, that Rebecca Kullberg was, in fact, my natural mother, and there was reason for them to maintain information on the Joan Crawford affair. The second she said it, she caught herself, and mumbled something like, "You can probably get copies from the Los Angeles newspapers."

I replied, "I already have them."

In December 1944, a strange event took place. My natural mother found out that Joan Crawford had a son named Christopher living with her. That was the name I had when I was a Crawford back in 1941. Evidently, she thought the adoption agency had somehow spirited me back into the Crawford residence in December 1942. On December 29, 1944, Rebecca decided to pay Joan Crawford a visit! The *Los Angeles Times*, (January 17, 1945) reported:

A wild scene was created in Miss Crawford's home, when Mrs. Rebecca Kullberg of 2017 1/2 Berkeley Avenue went there on December 29, 1944, forced her way into the actress' home, and ran through it, demanding to see "my son Christopher, whom you adopted two years ago."

Arrested at that time by West Los Angeles police, Mrs. Kullberg was questioned by both police and psychiatrists, and later released. When she was taken into custody yesterday by the FBI, which had reopened investigation of the case, Mrs. Kullberg informed government agents that, "An angel of the Lord" had told her that her son was in Miss Crawford's home.

I was nowhere near, and her efforts were for naught. I had been living with my mom and dad for nearly two years.

ReeAnn remembered that Andy and she were taken out of school by the FBI, and that the family was in a state of confusion for months after the Crawford Mansion incident. Rebecca was subjected to psychiatric tests and hearings, which she successfully outlasted. A subsequent article read:

Prosecution of Mrs. Rebecca Kullberg, 30 year–old housewife of 2017 1/2 Berkeley Avenue, for allegedly sending threatening letters through the mail, and annoying Joan Crawford, film actress, will be deferred, pending authority from Washington, to have the woman examined by psychiatrists.

This was the announcement made yesterday by U.S. Attorney, Charles H. Carr, who stated that such an examination should be made before the case is

brought to court, but authority first must be obtained
from Washington. Government agents charge that
Mrs. Kullberg sent a threatening letter to Mrs. Alice
Hough, welfare worker, and created a wild scene at
the home of Miss Crawford, where she went in the
belief that the actress had adopted her infant son,
Christopher.

Evidently, soon after the Crawford Mansion "break-in",
Rebecca decided to "rile-up" her perceived antagonist, Alice
Hough, out of frustration for not finding me at Crawford's
home. She wrote a condemning letter to Hough, who filed
criminal charges, which were in addition to those already
pending for the Crawford break–in. ReeAnn said her mother absolutely despised Alice Hough, whom she blamed for
losing me. It seems Rebecca was projecting her enormous
guilt to an emotion she could deal with, external blame and
hate.

Another article, in the *Los Angeles Examiner,* also
dated January 17, 1945, gave a good overall summary of
Rebecca's plights. It read in part:

Federal agents yesterday arrested Mrs. Rebecca
Kullberg, 30, on a complaint charging she sent threat-
ening letters to a welfare worker who once aided
Joan Crawford in adoption proceedings.

Mrs. Kullberg of 2017 1/2 Berkeley Avenue, also
was said to have caused a stormy scene at the
actress' home last December 29, when she appeared
to demand one of her children she believed Miss
Crawford adopted.

Miss Crawford denied that she had adopted Mrs.
Kullberg's baby.

The letter which brought about Mrs. Kullberg's
arrest yesterday, was sent to Mrs. Alice Hough, 135
North Van Ness Avenue, a voluntary welfare worker.

It threatened Mrs. Hough with kidnapping and bod-
ily harm, according to the complaint issued by Assis-

*tant United States Attorney, Charles H. Veale, and
implied that Miss Crawford also might share a similar fate .*

*Veale said that Mrs. Kullberg contended that though
adoption proceedings apparently were dropped three
years ago, after she protested such action was
"wicked," Mrs. Hough went ahead anyway and that
Miss Crawford obtained the child.*

*Refused admittance to the actress' home last
December 29, Mrs. Kullberg gained entrance by a
ruse.*

*Police said the Federal Bureau of Investigation was
called and Mrs. Kullberg was taken to the West Los
Angeles station, where she was questioned, given a
cursory psychopathic test, and later released.*

In her own way, Rebecca was becoming famous, making
a name for herself in both Los Angeles and Washington. It
didn't matter that the history being recorded by the Los
Angeles press, Department of Justice, and the Federal
Bureau of Investigation was sordid and degrading, only
that her life finally had purpose and meaning from what
was otherwise chaos and anonymity. She added color and
flavor to her character with such quotes as "Angel of the
Lord" and "wicked", and seemed to be headed for stardom
in this unsavory new light. Assistant U.S. Attorney, Charles
Veale, captured the essence of the matter when he stated
Rebecca's contention that though the adoption proceedings
apparently were dropped three years ago (November 1941).
Mrs. Hough went ahead anyway and Joan Crawford
obtained the child. It was interesting to note the reporting
practice back then of giving the ages and addresses of the
principle subjects. Both ReeAnn and Andy said their lives
were like open books to the public, and that strangers
would go by their house on Berkeley Avenue to see where
the lady lived, who forcibly entered Joan Crawford's home.
The Kullbergs had become objects of curiosity, much as
exotic animals at the city zoo, and Andrew Kullberg, Sr.

was not happy with his new fame.

The center of Rebecca's defense rested on proving that I had previously been adopted by Joan Crawford, which would show cause for her forced entry. At the final hearing, Rebecca offered as evidence a bed strap, which had been returned, along with clothing, toys and other personal effects. The bed strap had a Joan Crawford laundry mark. Charges were dismissed.

With all the publicity Rebecca was generating in the early part of 1945, I wondered if my parents knew what was happening. They certainly would have recognized the Kullberg name, as well as the first names Andrew and Rebecca, which my Mom had doodled and saved in the box. We subscribed to the *Los Angeles Times,* which carried all the stories of Rebecca's sordid exploits, her trials and tribulations. One such article, dated January 17, 1945, made front page headlines, *Woman Held After Row at Joan Crawford Home,* including a six-inch square photo of Rebecca and Doris Brown, Deputy U.S. Marshal. The staff at the Children's Home was aware of it, and I wondered if they might have called my parents to alert them.

I tried to leave no stone unturned during my information gathering activities. After reading the accounts of Rebecca's break-in at the Crawford residence and her mail threats, I sent off a "Freedom of Information" request to the Federal Bureau of Investigation. The FBI had been involved, but I couldn't tell to what degree. An attorney friend helped me with the request, which was a project unto itself. The "legalese" required for a simple "Freedom of Information" request was surprising. After dispatching my request, giving a detailed description of the events and names, I got a form letter saying I needed to send them a notarized signature, which I did. Then I received another form letter saying:

A search of the indices to our central records system files at FBI Headquarters disclosed no record responsive to your "Freedom of Information Privacy

Acts" request. If you know of any matter in which your name may have been recorded by the FBI, and can identify the matter in sufficient detail, including approximate time frame and location, a further search will be made.

The part that gave me trouble was *your name.* Should I use Marcus Gary Kullberg, Christopher Crawford #1, or my current name? I went through all that in my original request. I'm afraid I gave up on the FBI, and besides, I probably wouldn't get much more than the news accounts.

David Gary Deatherage at Harvard Military School, 1955

Floyd and Helen Deatherage,
Gary's adoptive parents.

David Gary Deatherage
March 6, 1944

Gary with "Bapoo," Gary's
adoptive grandfather, 1943.

Gary's natural mother, Rebecca Kullberg, with half-siblings ReeAnn and Andy.
Photograph taken in 1940.

Clipping from the Los Angeles Times, January 17, 1945

IN TWO PARTS

PART II — LOCAL NEWS

TIMES OFFICE
202 West First Street
Los Angeles 53, Cal.
MAdison 2345

CITY NEWS — EDITORIAL — SOCIETY

Times photo

SUSPECT—Rebecca Kullberg, left, seized yesterday as F.B.I. agents disclosed that Mrs. Alice Haugh, welfare worker, had received threatening letters regarding alleged adoption of Mrs. Kullberg's son. At right is Doris Brown, deputy U.S. Marshal.

Frank Mazzola in 1943,
Gary's natural father.

Current photograph of the
Mazzola Liquor Store near the
Berkeley Avenue Kullberg house,
where Rebecca met Frank.

Christina Crawford
(left) with Susan (right)
and Gary Deatherage
(center), August 1987.

Frank Mazzola with Gary

Gary and half-sister Haley Marie and half-brother Andrew Kullberg in Beaufort, South Carolina.

Gary and half-brother George Bauler (right)

Bill and ReeAnn Randall

Joan Crawford

It took a long time for me to believe that I was the adopted son of Joan Crawford, albeit for five months. Even with Betty Barker's firm conviction that I was the one, I wanted undeniable proof. Not until recently, after piecing the evidence together, was I convinced that Joan Crawford was indeed my mother.

The law firm's formal adoption letter, biographical sketches, and Mom's doodling of names, all preserved in the box, left no doubt that I was Rebecca Kullberg's natural child, Marcus Gary Kullberg. The June 13, 1941 news releases heralding Joan Crawford's adoption of a son, together with her autobiographical statement that the child was ten days old, tied in with my June 3rd birthdate. Alice Helen Hough, who was confirmed as Joan Crawford's baby broker by Christina Crawford and Betty Barker, handled my first adoption. This was verified by Penny Singleton, who knew Rebecca and had taken care of Andy and ReeAnn for Hough. The newspaper accounts of Rebecca Kullberg's conflicts with Alice Hough and Joan Crawford were in my file at the Children's Home Society of California, (CHS). Also, a representative at the CHS confirmed that I had been adopted at birth for almost six months. Now, when I behold my baby picture with Crawford, the likeness is true.

Not long ago, I was in the vicinity of Brentwood, an exclusive residential area of Los Angeles halfway between Beverly Hills and the Pacific Ocean. I decided to look up a place from my past. I was headed for a special residence. It was a Moorish house, located at 426 North Bristol Avenue, where many years ago, Joan Crawford and her children lived. This was my home the first five months of my life. I wondered how I'd feel when I saw it. I lived there from June 13, 1941 until just after Thanksgiving, 1941. I drove by it, maneuvering to the next street, which bordered the rear of the property. From there I had a good view of the house and grounds. It was both beautiful and fascinating. Somewhere on the second floor I shared a bedroom with Christina. Rebecca, my natural mother, had also been to this house to forcibly take me home with her. The Los Angeles police and FBI were summoned and had her removed from the premises.

I stood there for some time, daydreaming about what might have been. I wondered what it would have been like to play in the back yard . . . to swim in the pool which ran between the "Crawford Theatre" screening house and dressing facility . . . to belong there. I could feel the power of the house . . . it was beckoning me . . . it remembered me. A small part of me was captured within the walls of this house on North Bristol. It was a strange and memorable reunion.

In June 1987, I wrote and thanked Christina Crawford for her assistance and leads during the initial phase of my search. I mentioned that Susan, Mike and I would be in the Los Angeles area the second week in August, and if possible, would enjoy meeting her over lunch. I knew she was a busy lady, with the chances being slim for a reunion, and forgot all about it. Then I received good news from her:

Thank you for your letter—what a very strange set of circumstances we all find ourselves in at this point. My natural curiosity is such that I welcome the opportunity to meet you and your wife during your Los Angeles visit. What an unusual reunion this will be! I can hardly wait!

When I first met Christina as an adult, she was different from what I had expected. We had just parked our rental car, and Sue, Mike and I were approaching her front door when she suddenly greeted us from behind. She was warm, friendly and much prettier than the photos I'd seen of her. She has a radiant personality and a wonderful smile. I felt completely at ease with Christina, just minutes after her warm welcome. We all did. She invited us into her home and we talked. She started the conversation with, "Well, brother, tell me your story." As we got settled, I could hear her Dobermans barking and she went to quiet them. I glanced around the living room, and there was a massive oil painting that covered an entire wall. It was a dark classical work, a "Rembrandt" style, and set a rather somber atmosphere to the room. The striking thing was the contrast of the painting with Christina, who is blonde, blue-eyed and fair-skinned. She sat with the painting in the background, and her presence illuminated the room.

For an hour or so, I briefly told her my story. Christina would occasionally ask questions and volunteer information as I went through my journey. When I arrived at the part relating to my short life with Joan Crawford, she told us about the Brentwood house and relived some of our childhood. Christina mentioned that she and I shared a bedroom, and promised to send me a picture of it. She told me I should be most thankful that I escaped Joan Crawford's clutches! I responded that the situation might have been different if my natural mother had left me with Joan. I asked if it was possible that my presence might have changed Joan? Was there anything that could have altered fate?

Christina looked at me, and with much conviction declared, "It would have made no difference." She said, "I had it bad with my mother, but Chris' life was ten times worse! My mother especially despised males. Her father, brother and husbands were all hated and discarded. Chris was not spared her damnation." Christina repeated, "Just be thankful you were spared."

When Christopher Crawford was a baby, his mother adored him. He had a cherub face and was loved by all. He had everything he wanted until he was five or six years old.

His troubles started when he started to display boy/mascu-line traits. Any male tendencies were trounced on by Joan. Christina remembered Chris being damn near killed by her mother several times. That brought on his frequent desire to run away from home. During his school years, Chris went to many private schools. Christina mentioned Harvard Military, the same school I attended! I didn't remember hearing of him. I have since confirmed that he was at the school the same time I was, but was several years younger and didn't stay long.

In Bob Thomas' *Biography of Joan Crawford,* there is a passage that touches on Christopher's predicament:

> *Christopher seemed to suffer the most. Robert Preston was a next-door neighbor for eight years. Often, when he drove out of his driveway in the early morning on his way to the studio, he found Christopher standing at the curb. It was too early for his school bus, but the boy seemed to station himself there for a talk with his neighbor, such was his need for male companionship.*

Was loneliness what drove Christopher to his fre-quent runaway jaunts? Or was it a sense of not belonging that spurred him on? The young lady at the *Los Angeles Times* sent me about a dozen articles that chronicled his plight over a seven year period. Many of the news items narrated Christopher's efforts to run away from his home at 426 North Bristol Drive, Brent-wood. The last day of March 1951, he began his career of running. The *Los Angeles Times* broke the story on April Fool's Day, 1951, under the headline, *"Son's Runaway Prank Alarms Joan Crawford."*
The piece read:

> *Joan Crawford reported to police yesterday that her adopted son Christopher, 9, had disappeared, but*

the youngster was found less than four hours later.

The boy said he "ran away from home because I couldn't have chocolate sauce on my ice cream."

Said the actress at Columbia Broadcasting Studios, where she was rehearsing a broadcast: "He's not going to sit comfortably for a good many days after I get through spanking him."

Miss Crawford's excited call to police sent radio patrol cars through the hills back of her secluded Brentwood estate at 426 North Bristol Drive in a widespread search for the youngster.

He is the second of Miss Crawford's four adopted children.

The others are Christina, 11, and Cynthia and Cathy each 3.

After a three-hour search, he was found playing with two other boys in a yard several blocks away. The chocolate sauce episode occurred at lunchtime, when his frightened nurse called Joan Crawford, who was auditioning at CBS Studios.

Another news account related some of the dialogue between Joan Crawford and her son, which took place later that day. The conversation went:

"Hello, son," Joan smiled sweetly. She patted the sofa beside her, and Christopher came over to sit down.

"Hello Mommy," came the response. All charm. But Joan, who herself has won an acting honor or two, refused to be so easily disarmed.

Joan began smoothly, "Do you realize what you've done?

How many people you've upset and hurt? And over what? Chocolate syrup, indeed! You're lucky to have the ice cream!"

Tears brimmed in Christopher's eyes, as the lecture continued. "You may choose your punishment,"

Joan said. "What would you do if our positions were reversed and I ran away because I couldn't have chocolate syrup?"

A small voice from Christopher, "I wouldn't allow you privileges."

"So be it," decreed Joan. Christopher arose, all manners again, to take his leave. "Just go upstairs, son," Joan directed. "I'll be up shortly," she added, "with the hairbrush. I'm going to tan your hide and you'll take it like a guy."

So—like a guy—Christopher turned to go up the stairs.

I thought back on my childhood days at home. At first I didn't recall that I ever had such plans to run away, but then remembered an incident or two. I don't know what the occasions were, but they probably weren't much different from the "chocolate sauce" episode. I can remember Mom and Dad offering to help me pack, which had a diffusing effect, and I didn't make good my threat to leave. I never discussed such runaway journeys with my friends, but suspect the idea wasn't uncommon.

There were other so-called runaway attempts. In September of the same year, Chris took off. In the article, Christopher was reported to have said that running away from home was a good way to get his picture in the newspaper. In July 1955, while his mother was spending a honeymoon in Europe with her fourth husband, A. N. Steele, a liquor store owner called the police when Chris tried to change a hundred dollar bill—hardly worth mentioning—but still, the event made the newspapers.

In May 1958, Christopher was involved in a more serious incident when he and three others went on a "Joy Ride—Air Rifle Spree," shooting windows and street lights. A bystander was hit in the face with a pellet and charges were filed. That landed him in a private school for delinquent and disturbed children. Children's Court Judge Franklin T. Voelker said, "The action was taken at the request of Joan Crawford and her husband, Alfred N. Steele, President of Pepsi–Cola Co."

Was there a flaw in Christopher's character? Or was he driven to such ends by his mother? He had all the advantages a child could ask for, and yet seemed bent on throwing it all away. Did he require more love than Crawford could provide or had time to give?

Chris' problems grew to the extent that he eventually became a ward of the state at age sixteen. Christina said he lived with her in New York for awhile. Joan Crawford couldn't get at him. His mother never did anything more for him. No college education. No financial help. Christina says her brother has ended up a broken man. He is pretty much of a recluse now. He lives in a small town, does some kind of maintenance work, and has a family. The people like him in his small town.

Would my life with Joan Crawford have been any different? If life was as difficult as Christina pictures it in her book, *Mommie Dearest,* then I was lucky in the eventual outcome. However, at first, it was like going from the frying pan into the fire, when I lived with the Kullbergs. Knowing my personality and disposition, I probably would have tried to fight Joan Crawford and would have ended up with a similar fate.

Christina was very interested in how I was adopted. She knew the name Alice Hough, the baby broker, who helped Crawford get children. She also knew my natural father was Italian and that he owned a liquor store. Christina had been told by a movie producer that he thought her adoption involved Mafia connections. She was fascinated with the possibilities. Christina has never located her natural parents.

We had lunch at a nearby restaurant and came back to her home. She gave us a tour of her rambling home, and an autographed copy of her latest book, *Black Widow.* She mentioned that she's working on a new nonfiction project, which she hopes to finish soon. Just as we were getting ready to leave, I mentioned that my natural mother, Rebecca Kullberg, thought I was Elvis Presley. Christina gave me the strangest look and said, "I know that woman, she has written me!" Christina couldn't recall the letter in detail, except that it did talk about Joan Crawford, Alice Hough and Elvis Presley, and something about everyone was an idolater and going to rot in hell! I said to myself, "That's my mother!"

We said our good-byes.

> *Dead. Joan Crawford. New York City. May 10, 1977, at 10 a.m.*
> *Eastern Daylight Time. Official cause of death: Coronary arrest.*

So began Christina Crawford's book, Mommie Dearest, a diary of her tormented life with her mother, Joan Crawford. Page after page of sordid episodes were chronicled for the world to see Joan Crawford through the eyes of her oldest adopted daughter. A shocked public bought the book in record numbers, pushing it to "Best Seller" status. Reading the book, there was no doubt that Joan Crawford's purpose was to make Christina's life a living hell. The book ended with the reading of the will, a section of which read:

> *It is my intention to make no provision herein for my son, Christopher or my daughter Christina for reasons which are well known to them.*

Joan Crawford's two other children were contained in the will. All others who were a part of Joan Crawford's life, such as her loyal secretaries, shared in her inheritance. Christina's legacy was manifested at the top of the paperback cover, which read, *"The 3,000,000 Copy Best Seller!"* Also, there were eventual movie royalties. Joan Crawford will never be able to give her side of the story.

All of us can remember seemingly cruel acts by our parents, which in retrospect are understood as necessary and justified, or mistakes, which no one is exempt from. I know I have made dumb mistakes in the process of raising my sons, and can only hope they will understand over time. When I was eight, my mom sewed sandpaper in the knees of my pants, with the rough side toward my knees and inside my pants. She had heard that would keep the pant-knees from wearing through so quickly. Unfortunately, she misunderstood. The sandpaper was to go on the outside of the pants, rough side outward. Needless to say, I came home with bloody knees and she was beside herself with grief. I teased her about that for years, until I realized it really hurt her. I understood she simply had made a mistake. Some of the stories Christina tells in her book probably were like that.

Of the several books and numerous news accounts I've read, most presented Joan Crawford as a well-intending, generous, loving, somewhat eccentric, hard-working single parent. Some reported her as a disciplinarian, but a good mother. I understand that a public figure like her would tend to get "good press," but still, there would be the Sam Donaldsons of the media, ready for hard questions and sensationalistic stories. I found only a few, even with the rash of runaway (Christopher) news articles. On the contrary, there were more like the following account, given by Louella O. Parsons, Motion Picture Editor, International News Service:

> *Miss Crawford deserves a great big word of praise for taking four homeless children to her heart and making them her own.*
>
> *She is very strict, but still a wonderful mother. In addition to the love she heaps upon them, these youngsters are now blessed with a wonderful home, the advantages of a good education to come and the opportunities to make something of themselves in life.*

Still, my interest lies in the highly hypothetical and intriguing question, would life have been different at the Brentwood home, if I had remained a Crawford? I had asked Christina the same question and she gave me an emphatic, "No!" I had asked Betty Barker, and she told me, "I think you would have loved being Joan's son! Just as Cindy and Cathy adored her." Cindy and Cathy were adopted by Crawford in 1947 as newborn infants. Betty said, "All you had to do was be a good human being, and I know you are, so I know you would have gotten along with her beautifully." She said Christopher had a bad streak in him, including a vicious temper. Betty Barker commented, "He didn't bring Joan much happiness." God only knows what might have been.

Not long ago, I had interesting telephone visits with Cindy and Cathy Crawford. Betty Barker had written them about me, and I corresponded with both. I was visiting Betty at her place in Los Angeles, and she insisted on calling them on my behalf.

When I talked with Cindy, she was intrigued by what might have been . . . that we were almost brother and sister. She explained that her brother and sisters all saw their mother, Joan Crawford, in different lights. She said, "My mother dealt with us individually, and our relationships with her depended on her temperament and mood at the time." Cindy seemed curious about how I had discovered my past. I had the feeling she would like to do the same.

Cathy was half-asleep when we called. It past midnight in the East. After a few minutes of general conversation, she said, "Gary, my mother occasionally talked about you for as long as I can remember. You were in her thoughts. She always wondered what had happened to you, and hoped you'd find her."

When I asked about her relationship with her mother, Cathy replied, "I hardly saw her—she was a very busy person. We had to arrange appointments to even talk with her." I mentioned that I was interested in contacting Chris, and asked if she could help. She claimed to have no idea where he lived. She had not communicated with either Christopher or Christina since her mother's funeral, and had no desire to ever contact them. Cindy had given the same impression—that she wanted nothing to do with her older brother and sister. Apparently, there were hard feelings as Christina and Christopher had contested Crawford's will.

Christina's account of her life as a child of Joan Crawford reminded me of my experiences when I was assigned to Officer's Candidate School at Fort Sill, Oklahoma. That place was pure agony for me. I was there six months, from January to June in 1964. One-hundred-ten of us began that ordeal, and fifty-one completed the school to become new Army Second Lieutenants. Most of us were green college graduates and the balance were prior enlisted personnel who had won appointments. It was the most comprehensive and grueling training program I've ever participated in. In all modesty, to make it through the six months was truly an accomplishment. There were times when I just wanted to get the hell away and quit. If one moved an eyeball at the wrong time, it was grounds for a tongue-lashing and fifty push–ups. I was married at the time, but of course I was sequestered in the OCS area, with only visiting rights (one hour per week) during the first two months. After that there were conjugal Saturday nights!

Christina tells about several middle-of-the-night "raids" by her mother, where she went into Christina's room at one or two in the morning, and literally tore her clothes closet and bedroom apart. One such "raid" was for not using the right kind of coat hangers. That kind of harassment was also practiced at OCS. There was "no excuse" for the slightest mistake. There was good reason for the training at OCS. To mold men into leaders capable of accomplishing missions under the most trying circumstances; war, life or death. I must admit that the OCS training was good for me, even though I despised it. Those six months gave me maturity and wisdom that otherwise would have taken years. I was in the best physical shape of my life when I graduated June 15, 1964. I left Fort Sill vowing never to return, and I never have.

When all is said and done, Joan Crawford's purpose and motivation were not clear as a parent. She was confused. From what I can tell, she had some good intentions. However, her consumption of alcohol and work pressures often short-circuited those intentions. She had come from poverty and had worked hard for her rise to fame and fortune. Why should her adopted children have it given to them on a silver platter, without blood, sweat or tears? If they had been her blood children, would the situation have been different? Parents are usually motivated to give their children a better life than they had. Some think Joan Crawford's children were initially publicity gimmicks. When they were little, they were cute and lovable, both to Joan and her public. Then time transformed them into adolescents. They did not grow into a physical likeness of her. They did not have her blood. They outgrew their positive value for public relations and therefore their value to Joan. Joan Crawford lost the chance to love and be loved by her two oldest children. What a sad commentary. Perhaps Helen Hayes, who was a long time acquaintance of Joan's, put it best when she said, "Joan tried to be all things to all people. I just wish she hadn't tried to be a mother."

REBECCA

Contact

ReeAnn, like her brother Andy, has not seen her mother in years . . . some thirty years! Her father had passed away twenty years ago. ReeAnn didn't know where her mother was and hadn't talked with her. She didn't want to. She said her mother changed when I came along. Rebecca had been subjected to shock treatment as a result of the Crawford mansion break-in, and ReeAnn felt it may have affected her. Notwithstanding, ReeAnn remembered her mom as smart, shrewd and calculating; a person to be reckoned with.

She mentioned Rebecca has been writing an autobiography for years, and that my story probably played a major part. I asked ReeAnn if she knew my natural father's name and whether it might be in the manuscript. She thought it was Frank, but didn't know the last name. Since he was a good "supporting" actor in Rebecca's life, the chances were good that he would be in the script.

She knew he was Italian and managed one of the family's liquor stores with his brother, and that was all. I asked who might know his last name, and she thought I'd eventually have to get that from Rebecca. I wasn't sure I ever wanted to talk with Rebecca. The thought of her made me uneasy. If I could find out without contacting her, so much the better. ReeAnn gave me the addresses and phone numbers of two half-sisters and an aunt and uncle who might be able to give me more information.

ReeAnn sent me pictures of Rebecca at various ages and baby pictures of Andy and herself. I could see myself in one of the pictures of Rebecca when she was twenty-one years old. The similarity was in the eyes. I look at those photos often. I was fascinated with my resemblance to a female. Until then, my genetic mirror had been my sons. Regardless of my apprehension, I knew someday I'd want to meet, touch and talk with Rebecca, the person who gave me life.

I called Aunt Sarah Ellen Allen, Rebecca's younger sister, who lives in Phoenix. She didn't know where Rebecca was living. She gave me a brief history of her sister. She was a country girl from Indiana, (near Anderson), who was physically beautiful and naive to big city life. She had married a local boy, but it ended quickly and she left for California. After arriving in Los Angeles, she learned a lot of things the hard way. The whole family was shocked at the circumstances which brought me into this life—and especially the Crawford adoption incident, which resulted in Rebecca's institutionalization. Sarah Ellen was amazed that I was "found" and warmly welcomed me to the family. She had me talk with Jean, one of my sisters, who came to live with them when she was three months old. Jean reminded me of ReeAnn in her easy-going manner and warm friendliness. We talked for a few minutes and closed by promising to visit each other.

I had an opportunity to see the Allens in November, 1986. I was recruiting at the University of Arizona in Phoenix, and Sarah Ellen and Woody invited me to their home for dinner. When I pulled up in front of their home, Woody and Jean were waiting outside and gave me a royal welcome. Woody shook my hand warmly and said, "You almost became our adopted son!"

That was news to me. Evidently, Rebecca had considered sending me to the Allens, but had put strings on the arrangement. I was to be returned to her at some future date. The Allens tentatively agreed, but Rebecca backed out. That was sometime in 1942. As it turned out, they adopted Jean many years later.

Aunt Sarah Ellen told me Rebecca was forever after them to return Jean, and accused them of stealing her. They took Jean into their home as a baby and formally adopted her when she was five. Jean remembered the day they went to the courthouse and the judge asked her if she wanted to have the Allens to be her parents . . . her answer was yes! This happened during one of Rebecca's nomadic periods. Twenty years ago her transient periods were so fluid and frequent, no one knew where she was at any moment. At that time, Rebecca was thought to be roaming throughout the south and southwest. After the Allens officially adopted Jean, Rebecca found out and came to Phoenix on several occasions to take Jean. Jean remembered Rebecca and Kathleen (her next older sister) coming into the J. C. Penney Store where Jean worked part-time when she was in high school. They approached her and asked why she wouldn't come home with them. Jean told them her home was with Woody and Sarah Ellen and she was not leaving. When they heard that, Rebecca and Kathleen started shouting and cussing at her, causing a real commotion, while customers and associates looked on. Finally they left, and Jean vowed that she would never leave Woody and Sarah Ellen. They feel it was a case of jealousy, and that Rebecca envied the stable life her sister had and was trying to disrupt it by removing Jean.

Their modest home was warm and inviting. I couldn't help thinking what might have been as we chatted that evening. There were many knickknacks and pictures on display. Their home felt comfortable and cozy. They were loving, salt-of-the-earth folks. It was fascinating to think that I was almost a permanent part of their home. Goose bumps grew on me as I embraced and bid them farewell that evening.

Before I went back to my hotel, my sister, Jean, insisted on showing me the sights of Phoenix, which gave us a chance to talk. Jean, thirty-three, is a delight to be with. She is warm, sensitive, soft-spoken and an excellent tour guide. After visiting with her for an hour, I felt I had known her for years. We ended up on top of a hill overlooking Phoenix and the panorama of the lighted city was spectacular. It was near ten o'clock and the hill was crowded with parked cars, complete with amorous couples taking in the view and enjoying each other. It was a very romantic spot. Jean has had a taste of life, and has an adorable little daughter to show for it. She was single, attractive both in personality and physical appearance, and if it wasn't for the love of my wife, I would have been tempted to pursue her that star-filled night. Ah yes, there was another condition, she was my half-sister! What an odd experience that was, to have felt a slight attraction, but realized nature's laws discouraged any such thoughts. Brothers and sisters grow up together with an innate understanding, but it was novel to me. It was like being drawn and repulsed at the same time, and was a new sensation.

She also didn't know where Rebecca was. I told her I was interested in finding out my natural father's name, and asked if she had any ideas. She said George Bauler, my youngest brother, who lived in Houston, was in close contact with Rebecca, and could probably find out. She volunteered to contact him on my behalf, but warned that Rebecca would probably become aware of my existence. I asked if she could discreetly find out my father's name from George. She agreed to try.

The Allens recalled hearing that in recent years, Rebecca had lived from one end of California to the other. At one point she was reportedly residing in northern California near Redding, and then had moved south, possibly to the Los Angeles area. She had supposedly changed her name from Kullberg to Saunders, her maiden name, and Rebecca to Leah or Reah. Also, there was a chance she was still carrying the name Bauler, from her last marriage. Armed with these identifying bits and pieces, I spent some time trying to find her. I would rest easier if I knew where she was. For all I knew, she might be too close to Dad. From what I knew of Rebecca, I didn't want her contacting him. I called my old friends at AT&T, the information operators. I tried Redding, San Francisco, Oakland, and Los Angeles, with zero results. It was rather tedious giving all the possible name combinations each time I contacted a new operator.

Some became impatient with me and I really couldn't blame them. It was becoming apparent that any hope of locating her rested with George or Kathleen.

How could I be so blind? It wasn't until Jean gave her warning about Rebecca finding me, rather than the other way around, that the real picture was coming through. My brothers and sisters had been shielding me from Rebecca, and not vice-versa! What an indictment that was against my natural mother! Their claims of not seeing her in years wasn't a ruse, but the truth. I just couldn't believe that a mother, in the venerable time of her life, and her children, could sever their ties. That was completely foreign to me. The separation seemed to be a reciprocal pact, with Rebecca keeping her distance as well. At the heart of the isolation was fear. Fear of what Rebecca had become, which bordered on the sinister.

Several weeks went by and I heard nothing. Finally I decided to call George. Why have someone else do my bidding? Jean said she'd casually asked, but hadn't pressed. I appreciated that, but told her I wanted to talk with George. She gave me his number.

I introduced myself and gave him a quick rundown of my story. He had wondered why Jean was asking about my natural father a few weeks earlier. He said he'd heard about me over the years, but that his mother is convinced her son turned out to be Elvis Presley. He didn't know how she'd receive this new bit of news. He understood my desire to remain anonymous to Rebecca. He said he talks to her three or four times a week. Coincidentally, he had just talked with her in the past hour. I was getting close. He gave me her address and phone number, and said he'd try to find out the name I was looking for.

Unlike his older half-brother and sisters, George was contemplative and relatively quiet. When talking to him, he let me keep the conversation going, otherwise there would have been little said. I asked as many questions as I could think of without divulging too much from my end. His answers were thought out and guarded. I said to myself, I'll bet this guy plays chess and later, when I asked his hobbies, chess was one of the first. I told him I played a little and we'd have to play sometime—and he agreed. He is in his thirties and has been going to school as a Pre-Med student, hoping to be accepted into the School of Osteo-pathics. His wife is a Registered Nurse and mother of four. I asked about the heated conversation Andy told me about, and George casually brushed that off as a misunderstanding, and that he was only a teenager at the time. George seemed to be an intelligent, smooth young man, and I couldn't help wondering what he and Rebecca talked about.

Two days later I got a frantic call from Andy in South Carolina. His mother had just called, and his wife answered, letting the secret out. Angela had assumed her mother-in-law knew about me and said something like, "Isn't it wonderful about finding Gary?" All hell broke loose! George had called Rebecca, asking about my natural father, and after being questioned, probably mentioned that some guy named Gary had contacted Andy, claiming he was her son. That's when Rebecca called Andy and received Angela's "good news." At any rate, Andy said Rebecca knew about me, and she'd probably be calling. Andy said Rebecca had suspected something was up with George wanting to know about Frank's last name. He repeated what Rebecca had told him, that my natural father's name was Frank Mazzola—with two z's. That certainly had an Italian ring to it.

Then Andy said, "Listen, Gary, be careful when you talk with Mom. She can be treacherous, and just might show up on your doorstep if you don't watch out." I told him not to worry—that I'd have my guard up. By the tone of his voice, I think Andy was sincerely concerned for my well being. He said, "Don't let her get you down, and call me if I can help." What an introduction to my first conversation with Rebecca.

I called George to find out what happened. At first he seemed surprised about Rebecca's call to Andy. After awhile, he said, "She probably just became suspicious and was fishing; she'll do that." George confirmed the name Frank Mazzola, which his mom had given him. He said, "She'll be expecting a call from you," and I thought, why not?

The Early Years

I called her in the evening, about eight o'clock, Texas time, which was about six o'clock in Sacramento, California. A woman answered. I asked, "Is this Rebecca Kullberg?" I told her my name.

She had a very low, raspy voice with a light Southern accent. "Oh yes. My son Andy says you think you're my son, Gary. You seem to have convinced him, but I think you are nothing but a fake and a liar! Who put you up to doing this to me? People like you are sent from Satan to cause anguish and hurt. You shall surely rot in hell."

The stings came fast and furiously. I felt like someone had just hit me in the stomach, and I was trying to catch my breath. I told her nobody had sent me, and that my only desire was to find the truth about myself.

Her first barrage had taken the wind from my sails, and I nearly hung up, but I was the one who opened the door to the other side, she hadn't. I owed her an explanation, and a chance to hear of my background and discoveries. I didn't want to be put in a position of having to prove anything . . . especially to prove to this woman that I was her son, when I wasn't sure I wanted to claim her as my natural mother . . . not that there was a choice, unfortunately. Once she heard my story, my obligation ended . . .there would be no arguments . . .the facts would be presented for her to consider and decide for herself.

I told her about the letters from the box. She was very intent and occasionally asked probing questions. Rebecca wanted to know about me . . . to verify that I was the one. All the facts of my life hit true: birthday, June 3, 1941; birthplace, Los Angeles, California; hernia operation,

November 1942; biological sketch of her, Frank Mazzola and reason for adoption; the name, Marcus Gary Kullberg; and physical description.

I asked her why she named me Marcus and she said, "I remembered the name from my Latin class in high school and thought it sounded nice." Also, I inquired why they called me by my middle name, Gary, and got no reply. When I mentioned the biographical sketch the Children's Home had sent me, Rebecca became agitated. She raised her voice, saying, "They're not allowed to give out information. How'd you get that!?"

I explained that they could give general information, but none that would lead to names or locations. That seemed to calm her. It was obvious she wanted to keep the Elvis Presley drama alive. I told her of my dialogue with the social worker and the Crawford articles being in my file. She let that pass without comment.

After I presented my story, she gave me bits and pieces of information, which I already knew. The interesting thing was her change of reference to me from the outset. Now her phrases started: "When you were little . . . I took you. . ." She knows I'm hers, but she has a big conflict, Elvis Presley. One minute she'd talk to me as her son, and the next as an imposter back and forth for thirty to forty-five minutes. I didn't have the heart to ask her about Fabian or Elvis at that point.

Again and again she asked me if I was a setup by her family to play this charade to discredit her. I didn't realize how deep-seated the Elvis idea was. She had been living it so long, and had told so many people, that I almost hated to wreck her dream. I asked her about Joan Crawford, and she said it was all true, and gave me more details. After about forty-five minutes, we concluded our first conversation. We talked two times over the next few months. It was inescapable, I realized I wanted to meet her, to see her. I was going to be in California in several months, but didn't tell her.

She fancies herself a religious person and says she's studied Catholicism, Judaism, Mormonism, Buddhism,

Muslim and Evangelical Protestantism. She admits that her past sins were grievous and many, but that God has forgiven her. She asked me if I was brought up a Christian, and whether my family and I went to church. When I told her yes on both accounts, she said, "Well, that doesn't mean you believe in God, Almighty." I told her we believe in God and steered her to a new subject.

Rebecca called me about a month later. She was her usual talkative and irritable self. I asked if she would tell me about her life, and she asked where I wanted her to begin. I said, "From your roots in Indiana." I settled back and took notes. It wasn't difficult to keep up because her style involved a lot of preaching along with the story. An incredible story.

Rebecca was born on September 28, 1914, in the rural district of Middletown, Indiana, as the second of eight children. She had a happy childhood, living on a two-hundred acre farm. She says she met her one and only true love when she was twelve years old, while in the sixth grade. In 1927, when she was thirteen, her dad lost the farm, due to some financial difficulties. I told her that was the same year my Dad came out to California from Kansas. They had to move and she never saw her boyfriend again. She hated her father for the loss of the farm and having to move. They settled in Cadiz, Indiana, where she graduated from high school. She did well academically and was an honor student.

Rebecca said, "My clothes looked so terrible . . . I never went anywhere during my senior year at Cadiz High, but still I had to go to school. We were so poor. I was a very unhappy girl. I used to walk the fields at night to get away from my dad, who I couldn't stand, and prayed to God to lead me through this life. I wish I had one of those nights again with my dad, I believe I would be very happy. We see things differently when we get older, like I am." Her voice was full of emotion, and I told her I knew what she meant.

Rebecca was married when she was nineteen, to a local man who didn't give her much attention. She says he spent more time with her father than her, even when she was sick. She divorced him a year later and stayed with her folks for awhile. She was drunk once, and her dad ordered her out of his house, so she wouldn't corrupt her younger sister, Sarah Ellen. I asked, "She's your sister who lives in Phoenix?"

Rebecca retorted, "How'd you know that? Have you talked with her?"

I told Rebecca of my visit with Sarah Ellen and Woody, and she was very interested in hearing about her sister. Rebecca wanted to know what Sarah Ellen had said about her. She says she loved her sister very much when they were growing up, but feels Sarah Ellen deserted her when she needed help. She pictures her sister as the conduit of hate and alienation from her family back in Indiana. She says she felt forsaken by her family.

Rebecca continued, "I packed my suitcase and hitch-hiked to California."

I asked, "You hitchhiked across the country to California by yourself?"

She said, "Sure, it was easy. I had plenty of offers and I was very selective who I rode with."

I continued, "But still it had to be dangerous. How could your Dad let you go? How long did it take?"

She replied, "Dad was furious with me, but I was determined to get back at him for kicking me out. It took me about ten days before I got to Los Angeles."

Rebecca evidently made the journey without threat to her safety, which laid the foundation for many other such trips later in life.

Rebecca arrived in California in October, 1935, and stayed with an aunt who ran a boarding house in the Los Angeles area. Rebecca says her aunt, who didn't especially want her, told everybody that her niece was a dumb country girl without vices, and had been married and divorced. Rebecca feels her aunt's "blabbering" made her a sex target. Andrew Kullberg was also a boarder there, and Rebecca says she got to know him by playing cards. They had

126

lots of parties at her aunt's boarding house and afterwards, they often played cards. Rebecca says she was an expert at cards, as were all of her brothers and sisters. Her dad taught them when they were very young, and she remembered her grandma scolding her dad, saying it was wrong. "They all laughed at Grandma then," she said, "but I understand now. Card playing is a sport of Satan, who deceives people little by little." She married Andrew Kullberg in March, 1936.

I told Rebecca that I loved games . . . that bridge was my favorite card game. She said she played bridge also, but cautioned me about card playing. She condemns card games because that's how she became involved wiht Kullberg, whom she holds responsible for a lot of her problems.

Andrew Kullberg was born April 13, 1895, and was about twenty years older than his young bride. They had their first child, ReeAnn, on November 13, 1936. Andy, Jr. was born June 13, 1938. Life was good to Rebecca those first four years. She stayed busy raising her babies into young children. Her husband was a hard worker and a good provider. They had a comfortable modest home at 2017 1/2 Berkeley Avenue. When she could, Rebecca took her kids to Silver Lake or Echo Park to play on the grass and watch the swans glide over the lake. Then 1940 came.

Rebecca became restless. She was still vibrant, young and pretty. She wanted a full life! Andrew was forty-five and she says his desires were waning. She was ripe for meeting a young man and having an affair. She tried to tell her husband . . . to warn him. He hung around with an older crowd from the old country. Rebecca classified them as stodgy people, who weren't much fun.

In the autumn of 1940, Rebecca struck up a friendship with a young man at the local liquor store not far from home. He was Sicilian and very handsome. His name was Frank Mazzola, and she had known of him for three or four years. He managed the neighborhood family store, along with his brother, Paul. Out of the blue, she asked Frank to be her lover. She says he was very surprised! He was one year younger than she. They made passionate love many times, at any opportunity. Her affair was more to show her husband that she meant business, so he'd have to change his ways. But, Andrew worked long hours and had no idea of his wife's adulterous activities. Rebecca had not been with Andrew for some time. She soon realized she was pregnant and knew the father was not her husband, but her Italian lover, Frank.

She kept quiet about her scarlet condition for about five months, but then confessed to her husband. She figured there was no other way. Her husband was a pure Swede and blonde; the baby's father Italian and dark.

Rebecca said that when she told her husband the baby she was carrying wasn't his, he broke down and cried for a long time. To stop him from weeping and carrying on, she agreed to have the baby adopted. He wanted her to tell him who the baby's father was, and she lied. She told him about someone he'd never see. One evening, soon after her confession, Rebecca said Andrew came home with a huge bouquet of flowers to show he still loved her. He also stopped by the corner liquor store to get himself a large bottle of whiskey. Evidently, he and Frank had had words! Rebecca told me it was a wonder that she wasn't murdered that night, since Frank told her husband that she had led him on.

Just before Easter, 1941, Rebecca was at Echo Park swinging her two little children, ReeAnn and Andy, with me also eight months along in her womb. Another woman was swinging her child and they started a conversation, as women do. Rebecca learned the lady's name and that she was a lab technician for a prominent doctor in Beverly Hills. She told her that she was pregnant with a child that was not her husband's, and would like to know how to go about having it adopted. The lady said that she had heard at her office that it wasn't unusual for "movie people" to give five thousand dollars for a nice healthy baby. She gave Rebecca the name and address of the doctor she worked for.

Rebecca went to see the doctor. He gave her the name of Alice Helen Hough, her address and phone number. Rebecca called her. She told me that from the very first she knew Alice Helen Hough was from the devil. The minute they started talking, there was a problem with how to pronounce Alice Helen's last name (Huff). It took them five minutes to get that straight. Rebecca loves to refer to her as Alice Helen. Alice Hough despised her middle name, Helen. Rebecca's hatred stemmed from having to give up her baby, and Alice Hough was a convenient target to blame. Alice was the evil one. Rebecca was the innocent and that's how it went.

Alice Hough came and talked with Rebecca and Andrew. Rebecca describes her as a small woman with dark hair, who always wore high heels and a hat, which bounced up and down on her head when she walked. Rebecca said, "Alice may be loved by Satan, the god of this present world, but the eternal God who gives life has no love for her, for she is possessed with devils."

Rebecca claimed that Alice Hough deliberately told her husband all kinds of lies and things to get him "stirred up" so that he would come home and physically beat her. This was intended to make sure she didn't forget her promise to give up the baby. Then one day Alice Hough took the entire family to a barbecue at Penny Singleton's home in Van Nuys. When they went over to the Van Nuys home, Rebecca had been told their names were Mr. and Mrs. Bob Sparks. She had no idea of the "Blondie" connection until she recognized Penny. They all had a good time.

By this time, we had been on the phone for nearly forty minutes. I told Rebecca we'd best stop for now, or she'd have the national debt for a phone bill. She agreed, and we bid each other good-bye. I figured I'd get the rest of the story when I visited her in a couple of weeks. Most of it seemed to follow the same story line ReeAnn had given me.

Rebecca let Alice Hough, her perceived nemesis, have one last tirade as we ended our conversation that evening:

"In the sight of God, according to the Bible, God despises, hates, loathes and finds all people like Alice Helen Hough abominable, despicable, detestable, worthless scoundrels. Foolish people think people like Alice Helen are good people to be admired and honored because of their evil riches. These people are blinded by the power of money and the devil. Can I make them see the truth? I have tried for years, but people seem to love the darkness, the evil, the hellish. Poor Alice Helen Hough will face the truth when she dies."

The majority of Indiana's population is Protestant. They are dedicated to hard work and self-determination, as handed down from their ancestors. They're predominantly white, native-born Americans, most of whom trace their ancestry to England, Germany, Scotland and Ireland. Rebecca's heritage is English and German. Rebecca's birthplace, Middletown, is just east of Anderson and northeast of Indianapolis, and based on our road atlas, looks to be a small rural community. Cadiz is about thirteen miles south of Middletown, and is located on a major east-west artery, State Highway 38. That was where Rebecca began her ill-fated journey west in March 1935. The effect of her emotional decision to go west is mind-boggling. She touched so many lives. As I stared at the two small dots on the map, they became bigger as my mind played over my natural mother's childhood there.

I had talked with Rebecca four or five times by October 1986. When I called, the phone rang no more than two times, and she immediately recognized my voice, saying, "Hi Gary," or "Is that you, Gary?" I made comment of her voice recognition once, and she matter-of-factly said, "We all have different voice sounds, don't we? I imagine she has spent alot of time by herself thinking about her past. She rambled over her story like it was well–rehearsed. Her room must be small, as the sound of her voice had a compact quality to it. She said she ate regularly, has friends and enjoyed life.

I looked forward to meeting her, and hoped I wouldn't be disappointed. At the same time, there was an uneasiness about meeting her. She had a quality that frightened me. She sounded like she might have, God forbid, a little of Jim Jones in her. In the meantime, I decided to try and get a lead on Frank Mazzola.

After the fourth Los Angeles information operator told me there was no listing for a Frank Mazzola, I debated whether to solicit help again from my friend at the Social Security Administration. I hadn't forgotten he was reluctant the first time, and had gone out on a limb to help me find Andy Kullberg. On the other hand, I would save countless hours if I could go to the "well" one more time. Maybe he found the procedure was easier and safer than he thought, and he'd consent to another try. I decided to call and thank him for his help, and casually mention there was just one other person I wanted to locate. I promised myself not to press for, or embellish on my desires. If he volunteered, fine, and if not, I'd understand. We had a nice long chat. I sensed that things weren't going well for him, so I didn't impose, but thanked him for his previous assistance. I contacted another old friend who was with the IRS, but he wasn't any help. Probably just as well, for I had no idea how dangerous this hunt would be. No telling what the fallout might be, and so on second thought, the fewer involved, the better. It wouldn't be long and I'd be in California, where I could begin my investigation in earnest, and seek out my natural father, Frank Mazzola.

It was a beautiful Sunday fall afternoon when I arrived in Sacramento. I had business on Monday morning and would be going back to San Francisco in the afternoon. During the drive from San Francisco, I debated with myself whether to call Rebecca. Did I really want to meet this woman who was an adultress; sold me off to Joan Crawford; yanked me back for a painful year at her home; had been arrested for attempted kidnapping by the Los Angeles police, and investigated by the FBI; denied me in favor of Elvis Presley; and was incommunicado with her own children? The answer was yes. She was the person who gave me life, and I could not deny that.

I called her from my motel room. I told her I was in town, and asked if she wanted to visit. She was anxious to see me. At first she was reluctant to visit me by herself. She wanted her daughter, Kathleen, to be there too. I had talked with Kathleen on the phone before and she seemed okay, so it didn't matter to me. She called me back and said Kathleen was still working. Then she asked me if I was safe to be with by herself. I assured her I was harmless! To that she delivered a wicked chuckle, and my defenses went up. She lived in a small town near Sacramento.

About thirty minutes later, I was driving down the main street of her town. Up on the left I saw her hotel as it loomed up above the other buildings in the downtown area. It looked to be forty or fifty years old. We agreed to meet in the lobby. She told me the hotel had many permanent residents, mostly retired folks. I parked in the lot behind the hotel. It was dusk, and as I walked to the rear lobby entrance, I remember thinking the hotel had a strange glow about it. When I opened the door, I was hit with a pungent, musty smell. The lobby was dimly lit and bigger than I expected. Several minutes passed before my eyes adjusted to the darkness. It was open–spaced and sparsely furnished. I glanced around and noticed an elderly man with graying hair and glasses, standing in a small glass-enclosed area, which I guessed was the front desk. His small area was illuminated like a booth on a quiz show, and the light stopped right there. He looked at me, giving me an icy stare. I hadn't moved a foot since coming in the rear entrance—I was adjusting to a different time zone and unfamiliar world. My anxiety was high, and after surveying the lobby area several times, I barely made out a figure of a person in the far corner of the room—the only person in the room. It must be Rebecca.

As I walked across the room, I could feel her piercing eyes on me and I started to sweat a little. It was a "Twilight Zone" feeling. She asked if I was Gary, and we shook hands. She didn't look like her pictures taken forty years earlier. I realized all of us change after forty years, but hers was almost a grotesque transformation, shades of Dorian Gray. She was very heavy and her hair seemed darker. Her eyes were searching for lies, but she found none. She said she didn't expect that I would favor her side of the family. She thought I looked much like Andy Jr., and others in her family. In fact, she seemed somewhat taken aback.

Rebecca was sitting in a straight–backed chair that had been placed just adjacent to a small couch where I was to sit. There was a walker in front of her that she used to assist her mobility. After standing for a minute or two, I sat down on the couch, and sank into its well-used flabby softness. As I became settled, I found myself looking up at her. From that angle I could see the profile similarity with the newspaper photo taken in January 1945, after the "Joan Crawford visit." All her facial features were rounded with no sharp lines. Her hair lay straight down, which gave her a plain and stark appearance. We made idle talk for the first few minutes and she had an expressive way of tilting her head back as she spoke. Every once in a while a person would saunter by, giving a curious stare our way. I figured they were friends or disciples of Rebecca's.

Our conversation was spotty at best, as we were each taking in every visual detail of the other. Her eyes were the same as in her picture taken fifty years earlier. The eyes truly reflect the soul of a person. The man in the booth was slowly pacing back and forth in his small area, watching me like a caged animal. After awhile, I asked her if she would mind telling me about my birth and continue through the time she gave me up in November 1942, and the Joan Crawford event in 1945. I also wanted her to tell me about Frank Mazzola. She agreed, but it took her awhile to get started. She was still very intent on studying my physical features. She noted that I have to watch my weight just like her, and she's right. Rebecca was really in a preaching mood that evening. It was hard keeping her on the story line.

My Story

Rebecca went to General Hospital in Los Angeles on the night of June 2, 1941, and gave birth to me about six o'clock in the morning, after six hours of labor. Later that morning, a nurse brought me to Rebecca. There were other mothers in the ward. One told Rebecca that her baby was not her husband's baby, but he was going to accept the child as his own. She thought, why couldn't Kullberg do the same? Rebecca told her that I was not her husband's baby. The other mother told her not to give the baby away or God would punish her. Rebecca sighed, "What will be, will be." Rebecca said that Hough must have heard them talking, because she was abruptly transferred to another ward. In the next ward, a Catholic nun came and talked to her about her baby. She said the nun talked to her about her sins, and she cried. Rebecca feels the "Catholic sister" bit was probably arranged by "dear old baby–stealing Alice Helen." Rebecca said, "She knew her way around in the baby-stealing market. Seventeen years of stealing and selling babies for five thousand dollars each; old Alice knew it meant bread and butter on her table for her to bring this job to a successful conclusion."

As Rebecca started her story, I couldn't help wondering just how much of it actually happened. This story was forty-six years old now. Lots of time for imagination to replace fact. Time for her to invent different endings that suited her own ends. Over the years she has attempted to write a manuscript about her life. I asked questions along the way to verify her story with facts that I had previously substantiated. It was like beginning a gigantic jig-saw puzzle. I didn't want to bend the pieces to make them fit. I didn't have a picture to go by, except ReeAnn's first version and newspaper accounts.

Alice Hough came to take Rebecca home from the hospital on June 11, 1941, when I was eight days old. Hough brought Andrew along with her. Alice carried me and put me up in the back of her roadster on a shelf so that Rebecca couldn't hold or look at me. My natural mother started to take me down and Hough said, "Leave him be." So, she left me alone. On the way home they went through Elysian Park. While she was driving, Alice said to Rebecca, "Don't you think you are lucky that you have me to take the baby? Your husband does not want this baby. He says he will take his children and leave you if you take this Italian baby home."

Rebecca asked, "What will I say to my neighbors when I go home without a baby?"

Alice replied, "Oh, just tell them the baby stopped breathing and died, and that I took care of the burial."

Rebecca told me Alice Hough had it all figured out. Probably these same words had been spoken many times over the past seventeen years while she had been in the baby adoption business. Rebecca told Alice, "I don't feel like talking to my neighbors today." So, Alice told Rebecca she could go home with her and stay until night, and she would bring her home later. Rebecca didn't disagree, so Alice took Andrew home, and returned Rebecca and me to her home.

Rebecca was taken upstairs and put to rest in Hough's canopied bed. During her rest, Joan Crawford came in her Duesenberg and got me. Later, Hough and Crawford supposed that Rebecca had seen all this from the upstairs window, which she hadn't. This version differs from what I heard earlier. She says she just wasn't that alert while at Hough's home. She said she was too upset about losing her baby to pay attention to external happenings. The fact was, her baby was gone!

Supper time came and Rebecca heard them all eating downstairs. Much later they brought up a tray of food.

Rebecca says she was fed with the leftovers, much like you did the cats and dogs on the farm where she was brought up. It was the middle of June, and the days were long, and so it was about ten o'clock before Rebecca went home that night. Kullberg had fixed supper, but she didn't eat. Hough had suggested, since their two children were still at Penny Singleton's, why not go and have a vacation at her mountain cabin for a couple weeks. All the food would be furnished, and she said it would be good for them to get away. However, Andrew had been off work most of the time Rebecca was pregnant, and it was impossible for him to take off any more time. The mountain vacation was off.

Rebecca had a tough time those two weeks after I had been taken, and before ReeAnn and Andy returned home. Rebecca desperately grieved for her baby.

Alice Hough sent a man over to the Kullberg residence on June 13, 1941, with "official" adoption papers. I was ten days old. Rebecca and Andrew, the legal father, signed. June 13 was also the day the Los Angeles newspapers broke the story about Joan Crawford adopting her new baby son. June 13 was also Andy Jr.'s birthday, but he was still at Penny Singleton's place.

The next part of Rebecca's story was confusing. Later, I surmised it might have been a charade. Alice Hough had Rebecca and Andrew meet her at the Union Train Station. She knew it was several days after signing the adoption papers, and felt it was about the sixteenth of June. Alice had told her the purpose was to hand the baby to the adopting mother, as she was taking the baby out of the state. The lady was going to go somewhere in the east. There was supposedly a law that stated the natural mother had to physically give the baby to the adoption mother before leaving the state.

Rebecca wondered why this was necessary. They had signed the adoption papers, releasing her baby several days before. Why did she have to go through this again? Maybe the papers they signed were no good. Her hope was rising that maybe she still had a choice. Maybe she'd just keep the baby!

Rebecca said she and Andrew were to be at the train station about eleven o'clock in the morning, as the lady with her baby was to catch a train thirty minutes later. Hough said the train was going to somewhere in the "mideast." They waited until about twelve-thirty or one o'clock before Crawford and a young nurse arrived. They came rushing to them from across the train station. Hough told Rebecca, "Hurry up, take the baby from the nurse and then give him back to the lady, as they have to catch a train!" Joan Crawford stood there trembling violently. Rebecca said she had on a mannish suit, with a hat and long veil. My mother took me from the nurse and could see that I had been crying, and was now asleep. All of them were afraid that my mother was going to want to keep me, so they kept urging her to give me to the lady. Alice said that the baby had just been circumcised and that's why they were late. Reluctantly, Rebecca gave me to Crawford. Rebecca says that the second she gave me away, the nurse and Crawford, with me in her arms, immediately rushed out of sight in the train station.

At this point, I stopped Rebecca and asked if she definitely knew and recognized this lady to be Joan Crawford. Rebecca said at that time she really didn't know. The veil had hidden her face too well. Rebecca said it was actually a matter of putting many clues together. When I asked Rebecca these questions along the way, she would remain completely composed and gave rational answers. Her replies were instantaneous, without hesitation. She knew her story well.

Rebecca asked Hough, "How can they catch the train when it's been gone for over an hour?"

Hough replied, "Oh, she has a Duesenberg and they will cut across the country." Hough steered her and Andy into a coffee shop in the station, to give the others a little time to disappear safely. Rebecca remembered having an avocado salad. She says Hough mumbled something about, "Why does she always wear mannish suits with a long veiled hat?" Also, something like "that was dumb" and some cuss words. Rebecca remembered reading in a movie magazine that Joan Crawford always dressed like that. Joan seemed to have a penchant for such masquerades as she carried out a similar feat when she went to New York to get Christina. In Bob Thomas' biography of Joan Crawford, he says; "In 1939 Joan travelled by train to New York incognito." A disguise was necessary, not only to escape detection during adoption activities, but to avoid her fans at such a personal time.

Over a period of several months, Rebecca says she became obsessed with trying to find me. The guilt of giving me up was unbearable. Also, I suspect she had visions of extorting wealth from Crawford. I asked if she had seen a news release back then that gave my birthdate and birth location, which Joan Crawford says she inadvertently gave out. I never got an answer. I have a feeling she saw it. However, Rebecca insists that finding me was due to a vision from God. She said, "I got the Vision and the Dream by praying to God about my baby boy, who was born to me on June 3, 1941. Everything added up. God told me where my baby was! I dreamed three different nights that Alice Helen Hough brought the baby back to me. When I woke up, a voice said to me, 'Joan Crawford has your baby!' " Rebecca put all her clues together and decided that the voice spoke right. She wrote letters to Joan Crawford and to MGM Studios demanding my return!

The Union Station business baffled me for awhile. Then it dawned on me. It had to be an act to throw Rebecca off the track of finding me. To make her think I was being whisked off to somewhere in the "mideast," as Hough put it. Hough probably couldn't believe Crawford's attire as a "disguise," and that's when Rebecca picked up on her mumbling at the train station restaurant.

Rebecca didn't get any responses from her first barrage of letters. She also tried to contact Alice Hough. Everyone was ignoring her. Rebecca decided to get their attention. She wrote a letter to Joan Crawford, telling her she was going to kill herself if she didn't get her baby back! Rebecca told Crawford that she meant business! Within a day she got a telegram from Crawford's attorney, Neil McCarthy, telling Rebecca to come to his office at ten o'clock the next morning. She went. Neil McCarthy told her that Joan didn't want her baby, if she wanted him so badly. He told her that Crawford was in New York, and after the Thanksgiving holidays, she would bring her baby back to her in California.

About a week after Thanksgiving, Alice Hough and another woman, who had her hair dyed a peculiar red-orange color, walked up the alley toward Rebecca's home, carrying a baby and a suitcase. Hough introduced the woman with the strange hair as Laverne, Joan Crawford's sister. Rebecca found out that Joan had no sisters, and later surmised, because of the likeness, it was Crawford in a disguise. Rebecca was given the baby. She took him and sat down in a big overstuffed chair, with her children ReeAnn and Andy sitting on the arms of the chair. Rebecca undressed the baby to look him over "real good". Alice Hough screamed at Rebecca, "Leave him alone until Laverne and I have gone!" Laverne sat on the couch and cried, occasionally shouting an obscenity at Rebecca. They had brought one small suitcase of baby clothes along. Most of the clothes were too small. Also, in the suitcase was a "sleep-safe" harness, with a Joan Crawford laundry mark on it.

They soon left. As Alice Hough was walking away, Rebecca heard her say, "People that don't deserve children get them, and those who do deserve them can't have any. It just isn't fair!" ReeAnn, Andy and Rebecca continued to admire the baby long after they left.

Rebecca's baby was six months old when she got him back. She says the day I came home was one of the happiest days of her life. She remembered that my appearance had changed since she had seen me when I was eight days old. She recalled that right after my birth, my face had been round, my eyes brown, and my forehead low. When I came home at six months, my eyes were dark deep blue, my face longer and my forehead higher.

Rebecca told me that once she wrote the suicide letter and McCarthy answered it, there was no way Crawford could keep me. It was clear Rebecca knew where I was. There would be no peace. I wondered why Rebecca was telling me this. It was almost as if she wished she'd kept quiet and left me there with Crawford. She wistfully asked me if I wished she'd left me there. I didn't have an answer.

Often, while Rebecca was relating her story, her eyes would dart at me, and I knew I was due for some preaching. During those sermons, it was all I could do to get her back to telling her history. At times, it was like she was possessed by another being. It was startling. She would become demonstrative, using body language. Her eyes would flash around with her hands slicing through the air for effect. It was mesmerizing. She had a latent energy within her that, when released, seemed to electrify the air around us. At other times, it was eerie and a little frightening.

When I relive those sermon orations, I can see why some would question her sanity. I did. All of us have insane moments, but hers came more often. She wants everyone to know that she's devoted her life to God. She knows she's sinned and her guilt is enormous. Her sermons are directed at herself.

After telling me about how her baby had changed at six months, she said, "I seldom ever dwell on these things of the past because the bible says to forget past injuries, for dwelling on them will cause anger and vengeance, and take you to hell. Anger, vengeance, hate, slander, pride, greed and idolatry are all spirits of the devil and we must keep them out of us. We must let the good, kind, gentle, loving, forgiving spirit live in us. But, forgetting the past is impossible when my enemies are always chasing me, pursuing me, giving me trouble and grief. It seems they won't stop until they do me in. I believe God wants me to win this war, now and forever! The devil's people must not win. The more battles they win, the more horrible, mean, hateful, cruel

141

and proud they become. I can't let the devil become more powerful. Help me eternal God!"

Andrew Kullberg came home from work the day of my homecoming. He didn't share the joy and happiness of his family. Rebecca says that didn't bother her until he started being "real mean" to her and the baby. He wouldn't let the baby near him. Andy and ReeAnn would take turns hiding me in closets and other places around the house. He didn't want me within eyesight, or to hear me. The Berkeley Avenue house was very small. My existence there became precarious. Kullberg hated the little "Wop" baby. Rebecca says that when they ate, I had to be clear out of sight. She said, "Poor little baby, he knew Kullberg hated him, and he didn't understand why. Kullberg was good to Andy, his son. Kullberg wouldn't let the baby eat at the table with us. So, I fed him first and that made Kullberg mad, so I had to feed him after we ate. I put the little boy out on the porch and he would cry while we ate in front of him."

Rebecca said I was a very sociable baby. I liked being around people. So, when she moved me off by myself, I would cry. That, in turn, would put Kullberg to cursing and slamming his fists on the table or walls. My future didn't look bright.

Rebecca and Andrew had heated discussions every day, concerning the baby, which got worse as the months went by. Rebecca suspected that Alice Hough was involved with her husband's rotten moods. She had heard that Alice visited her husband at the meat market. She would visit him in the evenings just before he came home. Alice Helen would rile him up so he came home "horribly mean." Kullberg's alcohol intake increased. Rebecca said, "Old Alice wanted that baby back!"

Rebecca became pregnant with her fourth child who was due the last of November 1942, just a year after she got her baby back. Kullberg got meaner as the days passed on. Rebecca worked hard. She said Andrew would come home and poke her in the ribs with his big thumb while she was cooking or cleaning. She said those pokes eventually became gouges. She had black and blue marks on the sides of her body. At night, just as she'd fall asleep, he'd jerk the covers off and beat her.

One night Rebecca was carrying me in her arms. Her hair was long, and Kullberg was behind, pulling it. Yanking it! She thought he was literally going to toss her around, using her hair. She was close enough to my baby bed to put me in it. She escaped from his grasp and ran into the kitchen, and pulled out a butcher knife. Her husband, true to the butcher's trade, kept all the knives razor-sharp. She shut her eyes and started flashing the knife at Kullberg. She severely cut his arm in several places and his blood was everywhere. He went to the doctor. This happened when she was eight months pregnant. Her husband left her alone for quite awhile after that incident.

Kullberg and Hough were working hard to persuade Rebecca that she should give me up for adoption again. She says they were not quitters. Kullberg told her that if the Mazzola people would help support "the little Wop," she could keep him. Rebecca said her husband knew it was an impossibility. A friend of Rebecca's offered to take her to Frank's home to see his mother.

In the end it came down to extortion. Rebecca never admitted it, but I think she and Kullberg had always figured I was a meal ticket. I'd bet she really didn't count on Joan Crawford returning me—that she'd receive some kind of compensation to keep her mouth shut. I was a valuable commodity during my days with Crawford. When I became "returned merchandise" my value plummeted. My life was close to worthless, and as far as Kullberg was concerned, I was a liability and a candidate for the next life.

Soon they would have all the expenses involved with having another child. Rebecca believed that the Mazzola family was rich and powerful. Surely, if a prince of the family was the father of her illegitimate baby, they wouldn't mind providing a stipend for his support. She reasoned that Italians were close family people, and blood was blood, no matter what, even if it was a bastard. And besides, she

143

hoped the guilt of responsibility would play on their consciences. After all, they were a good Catholic family. Rebecca looked at me and smiled. She remembered Frank telling her, after one of their copulating interludes, that his mother had always wanted him to be a priest. She laughed, saying, "He would have been a good one." She also told me he wanted twelve children.

One day they drove to El Camino Drive in Beverly Hills to the Mazzola's big mansion. Rebecca took me in her arms, and walked up to the front door. She saw someone peeking out from behind a curtain. Then Frank's brother, Paul, came to the door. She told him that she wanted to talk to Frank's mother. He went back into the house and was gone a couple of minutes. Paul came back and told Rebecca his mother did not want to see or talk to her! She started to plead, and the door was slammed shut.

Then Rebecca said something that struck me funny. She had wanted Frank's mother to see how much the baby looked and acted like Frank. How the baby acted like an Italian, waving his little hands, and when he ate, he made a lot of noise. Later, when I told Susan what she said, I thought she would never stop laughing. When our boys were young, I was very strict with their table manners. One thing I absolutely would not tolerate was eating noises. Smacking of lips and slurping. When I thought back on my childhood mealtimes, my parents were equally strict with me. I was a "noise-maker" as were our boys. It must be in the genes!

Having failed with mother Mazzola, Rebecca decided to take her case to Frank. Several days after the Beverly Hills visit, she took me to show Frank. Rebecca brought me over to the Eagle Rock store, where Frank worked on Monday nights as the relief manager. She said she'd hoped that Frank would have mercy on the poor baby. Frank said, "No." He told Rebecca that if she knew what was good for her, she'd best not show up around him again. Rebecca says they were all so desperately ashamed of her and the baby. She said, "Maybe God will be ashamed of them and shut them out of heaven. Pride is of Satan, the devil!" Rebecca threatened to take my natural father to court. She said Frank's "people" were in politics and in high places, and that he told her if she pursued it, the case would just be thrown out. Rebecca said, "But there is a higher court, presided over by the judge of judges, God Almighty. His sentences and punishments are worse and more severe than the earthly courts."

Rebecca said the time came when she was almost due to have her fourth baby, Hallie Marie, and Kullberg was getting meaner and meaner to her and "the little Wop." Kullberg told her if she didn't give "the little Wop" to the Children's Home Society, he would kill them all when her baby was born. Her husband could see she had no intention of giving me up, and that his threats fell on deaf ears. The time for her to deliver was less than two weeks away. Each day when he came home from work, Kullberg turned into a predator, stalking me through the house. My survival depended on Rebecca, whose strength was fading, and it was all she could do to fend him off. Then one evening, the middle of November 1942, almost one year after my return from Joan Crawford, Andrew Sr. came home early and started drinking. After several hours, his ranting, raving and fist-pounding were rising to fever pitch. The killer instinct was taking hold of his mind and body, and it was clear my life was in danger. The Berkeley Avenue house had become a living hell for me, and there was no escape. He could hear me crying and demanded to know where I was, but Rebecca refused. He stormed off through the house, shouting, "I'm going to kill that little Wop bastard!" He rushed into the bedroom where he heard my muffled crying and discovered I was hidden in the closet. Rebecca was close behind, but could do nothing but shriek and scratch at him. There was no time to get the butcher knife from the kitchen. Kullberg tore open the closet door and saw me coiled up in a corner, sobbing and cowering away from him. He snarled, "There you are—you son-of-a-bitch!" My time had come. His claw of a hand grabbed my leg, yanking me from the hiding place, and in one continuous motion flung me through the air, meeting the opposite wall with a "thud"! The shock and reality of what he'd done momentarily sobered him, and he just stared at the small heap of human flesh writhing in pain at his feet. He was stunned to the extent that Rebecca was able to scoop me up in her arms and quickly left the house. She rushed me to the Children's Hospital on Sunset Boulevard, where I was operated on for a ruptured hernia. She signed the papers to give me up for the second time, and never saw me again until now. Rebecca recalled how I cried as the nurse took me away from her. She never forgot the look on my face.

Aftermath

Rebecca went into labor a few days later and had her fourth baby, a girl. She named her Hallie Marie. Rebecca sadly recollected, "And the days passed on, as they always do. I kept busy with my new baby and didn't have time to grieve. I never stopped reading the Bible. The Bible has always been a comfort and blessing to me, especially in my days of distress. I left life in the hands of God. There was no other choice. I despised Kullberg with all my being from then on. Still, I lived with him, cooked for him and the little ones. However, love and respect were gone. He was drunk all the time. I accepted the fact that my little boy was gone, and didn't think of him too much. Just once in a while, I thought of him until the day I went to Joan Crawford's house."

Rebecca recalled talking to the woman at the Children's Home Society after she gave me up. The woman's name escaped her. I mentioned the name Staunton, from my baby records. She said, "That's it! Laverne Staunton!" Rebecca filled in the first name. Staunton promised her she would never know where the baby was going this time. Rebecca told me she noticed in the paper that the woman died a year or so later . . . as if that was her punishment for her promise.

Rebecca lamented, "Kullberg, Hough, Crawford and the devil triumphed over me. They hated me and my religion. Kullberg, Hough, and Crawford were all in the same boat. Their little minds were not on God and religion. They felt a great contempt for God and people like me, who they quickly labeled 'insane'."

Several years went by and life settled down for the Kull-bergs. Then one day in December 1944, a good friend of Rebecca's convinced her that Joan Crawford had me again! Deep down inside, she felt Hough and Crawford had planned my eventual return to Crawford's home. She was sure Kullberg had been part of that plan, by insisting that I be returned to the Children's Home Society.

Liz Mazzotta, an old friend of Rebecca's, who lived across the street, had something she wanted to show Rebecca. Her friend loved movie magazines and consumed them all. She had a particular magazine she wanted to show Rebecca. In the magazine were pictures of rooms in Joan Crawford's home. Liz wanted Rebecca to look closely at one of the pictures. She brought a magnifying glass to help identify details. Her friend told Rebecca she had seen her "little Wop!" They both studied the picture of a little boy, a man and a woman. Liz told Rebecca, "That's your baby!" At that time I was three and a half years old.

Sure enough there was a Christopher Crawford living at the Crawford residence in Brentwood. It was like a self-fulfilling prophecy for Rebecca. She always suspected this would happen. It had to be Hough's handywork! Rebecca was determined to meet this development head-on and with strong conviction. She decided to pay Joan Crawford a personal visit at her home in Brentwood, a surprise visit that would catch them redhanded with me. Unfortunately, Rebecca didn't know two vital facts. First, Laverne Staunton was true to her word, making sure there was lit-tle chance, if any, that Rebecca would ever find me. I had been adopted by people Rebecca would never know or sus-pect, and who were completely removed from the Los Ange-les area. Second, that Joan Crawford did adopt another son, whom she also named Christopher. He was blonde and quite different from her "little Wop". Rebecca was head-ed for her final downfall. She would never recover from this mistake, and it would cause untold agony, misery and grief, not only for her, but also for her children. Rebecca's life was following the storyline of a tragedy, not unlike those orchestrated by Shakespeare.

Rebecca used the city bus system when she went to the Brentwood area. She found out Joan Crawford lived on Bristol, and at first went south. After much walking, she realized she had gone the wrong way. Crawford's address was on the north side. Rebecca figures she walked about two miles. The mistake in direction gave her time to reconsider, but she was not about to change her mind. Fate had mapped and sealed her destiny.

Finally she arrived at the right address, 426 North Bristol Avenue. She went up to the front door and rang the doorbell. A black man came to the door. She noticed a side entrance that had been opened by a white woman. She headed for her door. Rebecca asked if Miss Crawford was home. The woman replied, "No, she left for work about six this morning and won't be home until late." Rebecca asked if she could come in and rest, since she'd been walking a long distance. The lady pointed at the dirty doorstep. Just then a phone rang inside and the woman went to answer it. Rebecca simply opened the door and walked in!

She saw the stairs and immediately headed in that direction. The woman grabbed Rebecca and caught hold of her coat. Rebecca's momentum was such that the coat came off as she went quickly up the stairs. She dashed into one of the upstairs rooms, which she figured was servants' quarters, as it was small. Rebecca said the black man came saying, "We's goin' to put yo' in the newspapers and give yo' lots ah publicity for dis!"

She answered, "Good, that's what I came here for!"

Downstairs, the white woman was calling Joan Crawford, the Los Angeles police and the FBI. After awhile, they led Rebecca downstairs into the dining room where she sat down on one of the chairs. The woman yelled, "Don't you sit on Miss Crawford's chair." Rebecca, who was heavy at the time, told them to move her if they wanted. Looking out a big glass window, she saw two policemen running toward the house. Their hands were on their revolvers, and they were out of breath as they entered the dining room. She

149

told them to relax, she wasn't dangerous. They laughed and asked what the trouble was. She told them she came to see her little boy. Pretty soon FBI agents came and she told them the same story. Later that day she was taken for psychiatric testing and then home. Rebecca says Hough wanted her locked up, but the authorities refused.

Rebecca wrote Hough a letter and mailed it on January 13, 1945. Rebecca told Hough she was going to expose her as a black market baby dealer. On the morning of January 16, 1945, Rebecca was in the middle of hanging a huge load of wash on the line when three FBI agents walked up to her at the Berkeley Avenue home. Two men and a woman. They told her she had to go downtown with them for an hour or two. They let her change clothes. While in the car, they told Rebecca the newspaper reporters would want to get her picture. The female FBI agent told her she had nothing to worry about. Just answer the U.S. Commissioner, David B. Head, truthfully, and he would let her go home.

One of the newspaper articles I received from the Los Angeles Times included a front page photo of Rebecca and Doris Brown, Deputy U.S. Marshal. I told her I saw the picture she was referring to. Rebecca gave me a disgusted look and said, "The media people tried their best to make me look horrible. I felt like suing them for defamation of character. All the big newspapers were represented. I didn't get to look at all the photos until much later when my friend Liz showed me. The reporters were constantly trying to agitate me so I'd give them an angry menacing face. That's what they wanted."

I said, "The media haven't changed much, they'll do anything to sell newspapers!" She agreed.

Rebecca's picture wasn't very flattering. The angle was a profile shot taken looking up at her and it was obvious she had on no makeup. She didn't have a chance to fix herself up, and her hair was straight, giving a rather disarrayed look. She had on a coat over her dress, with a rose pinned on her lapel. In contrast, the U.S. Deputy Marshal, Doris

Brown, looked like she just stepped out of a beauty parlor. The look on Rebecca's face said it all. It was the look of someone about to be crucified.

Rebecca had a tough time of it in court that day. She tried to discuss her problem with David Head, the U.S. Commissioner. As Rebecca put it, he screamed at her to shut up and get out of his court room and added she was under a fifty-thousand dollar bond. The charge was sending abduction threats through the mail. Her life was falling apart—there didn't seem to be an end to her problems. She had done nothing wrong. There wasn't enough money for a fifty–dollar bond, let alone fifty-thousand dollars! Rebecca said Kullberg was furious with her for making the front page of all the Los Angeles papers. His anger kept him from coming to see her. He had signed a statement, indicating she was criminally insane. Later, during court proceedings, he testified that Alice Helen Hough had coerced him into signing a blank form, which she filled in.

Rebecca was taken to the county jail, booked, fingerprinted, photographed, given jail clothes, ordered to take a shower, put in a cell and locked up. She remembered, as a senior at Cadiz High School, their principal took the senior class to the penitentiary for a visit; also to the poor farm, and insane asylum, as a warning for them to stay away from such awful places! Rebecca looked at me and smiled, "I've made all three." It took five days before she could sleep in the jailhouse. She was in the county jail for two weeks before given a hearing. Once it was determined Kullberg's "criminally insane" statement wouldn't hold up, they told her she was to be released. Rebecca was ready to go home. Instead, they escorted her to the psychopathic ward at General Hospital and locked her up again.

Rebecca gave me a taste of county jail life before delving into her psycho-ward experience. Every morning they got up at five-thirty and marched into the dining room for breakfast. The guards opened up the windows so they could see outside for a few brief moments. She said it was a blessing just to see the lights and traffic of the outside

151

world. In jail they had electric lights day and night. No looking outside. Prison punishment for the wicked. The meals were not fattening and tasted like cardboard most of the time. Occasionally there was music playing. Rebecca says she met and knew Louise, the convicted husband killer, who was in her cell ward. She was very pretty and called the "queen" of the jailhouse. Another woman had also killed her husband, "Shot him right between the eyes," she said. They all dreamed how wonderful it would be to sleep and eat well again. She said her cellmates had colored, beautiful pictures of food pasted on the walls of their cells. The food photos included ham and eggs, juicy hamburgers, milkshakes, barbecued steaks, and banana splits. Rebecca was anxious to leave—the two weeks seemed like two months.

After three days at the General Hospital psycho–ward, Rebecca received her sentence from Judge Valentine. He sat at a little table outside her room. That's where "court" was held. Judge Valentine sentenced her to Patton State Hospital for the criminally insane. Rebecca demanded a jury trial and the judge granted it. At the time the judge was "holding court," Rebecca was somewhat uncomfortable and immobile. They had given her booties and an old gray robe, and had taken her hairpins away so she wouldn't hurt herself. She said her hair was wild. She was belted to a rocking chair, which was chained and locked to the bed. Her arms and feet were shackled. She smiled and told me, "They had a red sign outside my door stating, 'DANGER; SYPHILLIS INSIDE.' " Her case was scheduled for the first week of March 1945; to be held in Superior Court, which was downtown Los Angeles.

The court case was short and humorous. Alice Helen Hough was called to the witness stand, and she was very nervous and agitated. There was a pitcher of liquid she occasionally poured in a glass and drank. She pleaded with the judge to let her go home as she was not feeling well. Rebecca's attorney spoke up and said that he would need her for cross-examination later. That made Hough even more nervous.

Rebecca told me Hough's testimony was revealing, as she counted something like fifty lies. Once, while Hough was testifying, Rebecca said she mouthed the words, "You are a liar!"

Alice read her lips and screamed, "Your Honor, she is sitting there calling me a liar."

Rebecca's attorney jumped up and said, "Your Honor, I'm sitting right beside my client and I didn't hear a word." Rebecca's attorney whispered to her, "Let Alice lie, it will help in the long run." It did. Rebecca didn't understand how Hough got away with perjury.

The most serious accusation was that Rebecca had come to Hough's home and threatened to kill her with a pearl-handled pistol. Hough claimed she barely escaped with her life. Alice Helen testified that she slammed the car door on Rebecca's arm, forcing the pistol to fall. Rebecca's attorney had Rebecca show her arm. There were no marks. That pretty much ended the case. When Rebecca testified, she told them about Crawford's first adoption of her baby and that was why she went into Crawford's home. She brought the "sleep safe" harness with the Joan Crawford laundry mark on it. Rebecca said the jury was in tears. She felt that her ability for persuasive speech had always been strong. Her ability was evident from her high school days where she participated in plays. She said her attorney told her that she had the power to make the jury laugh or cry.

They debated in the judge's chambers whether to call Joan Crawford as a witness. It was decided that her testimony wasn't necessary. Rebecca felt Crawford bribed them. No record of the court trial was in any of the papers. She thought Hough managed to stifle the media, but doesn't know how.

Rebecca told me she tried to get a court transcript. It was not available. I had found the same thing. I had written and talked with the records people at Los Angeles City Hall. Since it had been a misdemeanor, her case file had been destroyed twenty years ago. I was able to get the case number, which was evidence that it happened, but no file.

The jury brought in the verdict that Rebecca was sane and should be set free to go home to her family. The police woman, who had escorted her between the courthouse and General Hospital, told her that she would retrieve her personal effects. Her things were in another building. Then she would take Rebecca downtown to catch a trolley to ride home. She let Rebecca out at the psycho-ward so she could go in to get her Bible and what little else she had in the room. One of the interns, who had given her baths, saw Rebecca in the hall, and ordered her to get into her room. Rebecca told her that she had been set free by the jury and was going home. The intern screamed, "Oh, no you're not!" The intern summoned another woman, who helped lock Rebecca in her old room. She told me they beat and shoved her down the hall to her room. Finally, the policewoman came and rescued her.

Andrew Kullberg, Sr. wasn't happy to see her come home. He felt she was a disgrace to the family.

Rebecca has become paranoid over the years and still feels "government forces" are lurking to get her. She told me that "cruel forces" of government have given her a hard time for thirty-eight years, and she doesn't see relief. She claims to have insurmountable problems with the Social Security Administration. She had hoped that her story would get published. She said, "I know they don't want me publishing this story, which is the truth. So far they have succeeded. It seems they have unseen powers, but I have God and His power, which is greater than Satan's power. So, we'll see who the winner is—them or me, Satan or God." She said, "I am sure my enemies believe they can stop anything I write from being published. But my God's power is matchless. It will happen somehow. I am not able to know what the future will bring. I am not a fortune teller. If God was to speak to me again, and tell me things, I would know. But God hasn't spoken to me for many years now. I believe it's because it's taken me so long to understand that all of us are required to walk the straight and narrow. It is a hard thing to do in this wicked age. First,

one must survive. A happy spirit is necessary to live. I picture how beautiful and happy it will be in heaven, which we
are every day traveling towards, in our journey through life.
Like I thought to myself, when I first gave my third baby
away, I'll see him again in heaven. It was a very positive
thought, like God had given it to me."

The eerie thing is that if I succeed and this is published,
I will have told Rebecca's story, as well as my own. I will be
fulfilling her prophecy. When I wrote this she knew nothing
of my project. The more I dug into my past, the more I
thought about life and realized how little I knew about the
forces at work in this universe. I have increasingly found
myself pondering over and trying to conceptualize the
bounds and transitions of the continua; good-evil, reality-
dreams, sanity-insanity, existence-nonexistence, and
earth-universe-God. Life is indeed a mysterious force. I
wondered what God had in store for me and the purpose of
my existence.

I told Rebecca I had to be going soon, but wanted to
know what she thought about my trying to locate Frank
Mazzola, my natural father. Rebecca became very serious
and her eyes narrowed as she pondered my question. She
told me that if I planned to pursue the Mazzolas, I should
be very careful. She said they were Sicilians, and very
much part of the Mafia family! The family was in the liquor
business, having five or six stores, and was a powerful
force in the Los Angeles area. They had come from Palermo,
Sicily when Frank was a little boy of five. Back in the
1930's, she had heard of mysterious disappearances and
that the Mazzola family had been involved. She said Paul
and Frank had nerves of steel and were ruthless. They
would stop at nothing to take what they wanted. Rebecca
said she always felt the Mazzolas somehow caused her alot
of her problems over the years. I asked why, and she pointed at me!

As she talked, I had visions of a horse head on my bed
at home, or becoming an integral part of a scrap metal pile.
Now they probably have some kind of pill or injection that

causes increased cholesterol levels with sudden heart attacks as the result. My cholesterol level wouldn't take much. Also, "accidents" of one kind or another were probably still popular forms of elimination. I hoped submachine gun forays were a thing of the past. Maybe I'd just stop my search right there.

While we talked, a friend of Rebecca's brought over a large sack of vegetables and fruit. As our visit came to an end, I offered to help her take the sack to her room and she agreed. When she she got up, she wasn't much taller than when she was sitting. She was extremely heavy, but moved surprisingly swiftly with the aid of the walker. As we got on the elevator, she gave me a rather weird smile, something like, "now I've got you." We went up to the third floor, ever so slowly. When the elevator door opened, I was startled by a woman who suddenly appeared and gave Rebecca a knowing glance. My imagination started to run wild. Was I being set up? We walked down a long hall to her room. I was beginning to feel uneasy. In the lobby I could just get up and go, but now I was deep in the body of this structure where Rebecca lived. She gave me the key to open the door, and I took the sack into her room. Rebecca wanted me to wait while she called Kathleen, so I could meet with her. While she called, I looked around her small and crowded room. My eyes stopped at an entire section of the room that obviously had special meaning for her. An entire wall and table had been devoted to Elvis Presley! Stacks of newspaper clippings, pictures and memorabilia. Rebecca gave me the phone, and I talked with Kathleen. We arranged to meet at a restaurant. I said goodbye to Rebecca.

When I left her room and closed the door, I had an urge to get out of that hotel. The hallway walls seemed to close in on me. The elevator took forever. When I finally reached the first floor, I was running through the lobby. Outside it was pitch black. I got into my rental car and fumbled for the car keys. There was another strange key in my pocket. It was the key to Rebecca's room. Damn! How did it get there? I must have inadvertently taken it when I opened her door. I had to force myself to go back in the hotel. It reminded me of the lodge in Stephen King's, *The Shining.* I dropped the key off at the desk and told the man I had mistakenly put it in my pocket. He gave me a penetrating stare that added to my uneasy feeling. I quickly left.

As I drove back to Sacramento, I thought about the wild life Rebecca had. She lamented over her life with her husband, Andrew. He was twenty years her senior. His demeanor and attitude were from the "old school." She was still a young woman, full of vitality, while he was rapidly becoming an old man both physically and mentally. She was trapped. Fate destined her for tragedy. After my birth and all the repercussions, she was exiled to a life without close family or a home. She hitchhiked across the United States several times with children in hand. She would move from place to place at the slightest provocation. The momentum of this lifestyle accelerated as the years went on. George, her youngest, attended over thirty different schools before he graduated from high school!

Whether real or not, she felt "evil" forces have been against her since my birth. She has a definite persecution complex. Rebecca fit the symptoms of a paranoid schizophrenic. She felt Joan Crawford and Alice Hough were forever trying to take revenge. She imagined the Mazzola family was after her for attempting to pawn me off on them. Last, but not least, she thought her family in Indiana was trying to hurt her for disgracing the family name. When I surfaced, she suspected I was an agent being paid to wreck what life she had left.

After a few missed turns, I found the restaurant where I was to meet Kathleen and her husband for dinner. Sacramento wasn't a difficult city to navigate, and I'd been there many times visiting George and Pat Deatherage, but my mind was replaying Rebecca's story, which had dulled my sense of direction. When I talked with Kathleen from Rebecca's room, she had surprised me by saying my brother George Bauler was visiting and would be joining us for dinner. Before I left, Rebecca had shown me a picture of

Kathleen, so I'd know who to look for.

As I was parking at the restaurant, I recognized Kathleen emerging from another car six spaces away. Kathleen's husband, Floyd, and George followed close behind her. We walked toward each other as we approached the restaurant entrance. I waved and Kathleen pointed simultaneously. We greeted each other and went in. It was late, and I was the only one who hadn't eaten. I ate a sandwich, while the others drank coffee. We had a good visit, trading stories and getting to know each other. I didn't think of it at the time, but that was a peculiar reunion. We were Rebecca's three "non-Kullberg" children, all with different fathers. What a strange group we were, being brother(s) and sister, with a resemblance factor near zero. Rebecca's variant taste in mates made sure of that. After dinner we went to Kathleen's for drinks, and a trip through the family photo albums. It was an interesting and enjoyable visit and I didn't get back to my room until after midnight.

I wrapped up my business in Sacramento by noon on Monday and headed back to San Francisco. I had been up until two o'clock that morning, putting down everything I could remember about my chat with Rebecca. As I drove along, yesterday seemed like such a long time ago, with everything taking on the aspect of a dream. Was I experiencing a hallucination or reality? Did I really touch and talk with the person who gave me life? I had the sense to copy Rebecca's colorful story of our early life together before sweet sleep took hold. I can recall objective information like facts, figures and conceptual relationships, but subjective memory is another matter, like languages and memorizing passages. For that reason, I wasn't able to recall all of Rebecca's innocuous sermons. Those I penned were constructed as close to a verbatum account as possible.

I was anxious to stop for lunch at the Nut Tree, where I could read over my notes a few times. Rebecca's life was a tragedy, whether self-inflicted or otherwise. Each turning point whisked her from one nightmarish journey to another. What would have been a "cold sweat" dream for me, was everyday reality for Rebecca. Thank God I was spared that miserable existence!

I arrived in San Francisco late afternoon and checked into my hotel with a bay-view room. After several business appointments I relaxed in my room with a Scotch. I called David at UC Berkeley and set a dinner date for the following evening. After finishing my drink, I ate dinner at the hotel and reviewed my business schedule for the next day. Before turning the light out, I looked over my notes from yesterday's visit with Rebecca.

I had completed a full day when David joined me in my room for cocktails. We sat and talked for several hours before going to a Chinese restaurant. I told David about my visit with Rebecca and he listened attentively. He was probably trying to figure his dad out. What was this all-consuming compulsion to raise the dead? Things were great the way they were. In his wisdom, he let me ramble on, which helped cleanse my soul. The guilt of unearthing the past and not telling my dad weighed heavily on my conscience. After dinner we bid farewell.

Elvis

Elvis Presley was born January 8, 1935, in Tupelo, Mississippi. He was the focus of wild adulation among the young in the mid 1950's. While working as a truck driver in Memphis, Tennessee, he made a few records at a local studio and was soon a popular country and western singer, touring with a show throughout the south. He also sang rhythm and blues, which eventually became his hallmark. A major recording contract followed in 1955; in 1956 his first big hit, *Heartbreak Hotel*, was released, which was soon just one of many. Songs like *Hound Dog, Don't Be Cruel, Love Me Tender,* and *All Shook Up* sold millions of copies, and Presley's life and television appearances attracted mobs of screaming teenagers. The pronounced gyrations, which accompanied his singing and earned him the title, *Elvis the Pelvis,* drove his audiences to heights of frenzy. Others roundly denounced his music as signs of moral decay. His popularity continued unabated in motion pictures through the 1960's, when he starred in from one to three each year.

From the first time I talked to Andy, there has been a subliminal reference to Rebecca's belief that Elvis Presley was her lost son. Fabian was in that hallowed position in the earlier years until his popularity faded, prompting Rebecca to find an idol whose legend would live on with her. It wasn't until I saw the "Elvis Shrine" in her hotel room, that I realized the ghost of Elvis Presley was a big part of her life. I collected and put together bits and pieces of Rebecca's fairytale, so that I could better understand her psyche. Her efforts to make the tale come alive were pathetic at best.

Rebecca's biggest hurdle was to explain away the six and a half years difference in birthdates, January 8, 1935 to June 3, 1941. She attempted to accomplish this by saying there was a conspiracy to make Elvis older than he actually was because of child labor laws. She says they didn't want the public or authorities to think Elvis was being forced to perform as a child for the profit of others. Several acquaintances supposedly verified that he was much younger than his stated years. One such witness was a woman Rebecca boarded with in Memphis for about two weeks, back in 1974. The woman said she went to parties at Graceland with Elvis, having been a schoolmate of his. She agreed with Rebecca's insistence that he was six years younger. Rebecca's case rested on several such corroborations. She feels all the authors who wrote about Elvis were bribed to lie about his age.

Rebecca gave "birth" to Elvis when she went to Graceland, Elvis Presley's home, with a sightseeing tour. She found out quite a bit about him. He had given huge sums of money to the Catholic orphanage at Christmas time, and had been managed by a certain Colonel Tom Parker. She studied Vernon and Gladys Presley, reading anything and everything she could put her hands on. Albert Goldman's book on Elvis was a favorite, as he brought up questionable segments of Presley's life, which Rebecca has twisted (really contorted) to suit her ends. As she said, "If you dig hard enough, the truth will come out." Once, while waiting at a bus stop in Memphis, she struck up a conversation with a stranger who said his sister dated Elvis, and that Presley had told them he was taken from an orphan's home. That's all Rebecca needed to hear, and her imagination ran rampant.

All her old nemeses came back into focus; Joan Crawford, Alice Helen Hough, and the Children's Home Society. Now it was clear that Hough had supervised the transfer of Rebecca's son to the Catholic Orphanage in Memphis, where the Presleys adopted him. Joan Crawford was involved too, as she was the financial backing for the whole scheme, to include raising Elvis to be a superstar. Colonel Parker, in Rebecca's eyes, was the coach, a slave-driver and user—from the same stock as Alice Hough, an agent for the devil. Rebecca said she went back to Graceland on her own to talk with the gate guard, or whoever was around. She initiated a conversation with the gateman, and told him right off she was Elvis Presley's real mother. The man evidently didn't argue with her, which was tantamount to agreement in Rebecca's mind. The gateman told her Elvis was darker than she, to which she explained the father was Sicilian Italian. He said she should come back and visit with Elvis when he returned July 4, 1974. Rebecca told me she never went back because she knew "evil forces" would be waiting for her.

I asked, "Who?"

Rebecca replied, "Colonel Tom Parker is said to possess hypnotic powers. That alone revealed that he is possessed with the evil spirits of Satan, but he wasn't the only one. Parker had others telling him what to do. Like Alice Helen Hough, Joan Crawford, and the Children's Home Society of California. People just can't understand Elvis' situation without a little deep thought." She continued, "Satan's people are very secretive, sneaking, conniving, and thriving with their bags of little dirty tricks. They say one thing and mean another. You can't believe a word they say. Liars, thieves, idolaters, hypocrites, scoundrels; they all have the same father. Satan, a mighty busy man."

Rebecca wondered if the Presleys were related to Alice Hough, and supposed she helped them dream up some of the lies written about the ancestry of Elvis, as detailed in Albert Goldman's book. She felt that the truth of the adoption would come out someday, revealing the true parents and ancestors of Elvis. Rebecca said, "When you read these books with eyes like mine, you see many things that just don't look and sound right." She told me Goldman's book hints all the way through it that there was a mystery about Elvis' birth and death.

Once, during a phone conversation, I asked, "Why do

you live this lie about Elvis Presley being your son? You know it isn't true!" There was a long pause, and I felt bad. What could she say? She has told so many! How can she save face? All her family treat the subject with embarrassment and brush it off.

Just a few comments about Fabian, who Rebecca originally tried to cast as her long-lost child. Fabian Anthony Forte was born February 6, 1943, in Philadelphia, Pennsylvania. He was the first of three sons born to Joseph and Dominic Forte, who were of Italian ancestry. The Italian heritage would have agreed with Rebecca's plan. He was about eight years younger than Elvis and only nineteen months away from my birthday. Rebecca's effort to rationalize the age difference, was probably easier than with Elvis, but Fabian's birth facts don't seem to be as mysterious or pliable as Presley's. Notwithstanding, Fabian's rise to fame, in the style of Elvis, was not sustained and he fell back to mere mortal status, which prompted Rebecca to seek out the master, Elvis.

Rebecca's life has been such a disaster, and my birth was the turning point. Over the years, she needed something bigger than life as the propitiation of all that went wrong. It was natural for her to focus on me and try to transform the object of her pain into an idol or something god-like. In effect, to make all her tragedies be worth it. To visualize me as a Fabian or Elvis fulfilled those needs.

MAZZOLA

The Search

After completing my business in San Francisco, I flew to Los Angeles to spend a day visiting the places of my past. My sister ReeAnn and her husband Bill had invited me to use their home as headquarters during my stay. It was my first chance to see and touch ReeAnn since my abrupt departure from the Berkeley house forty-four years earlier. I wanted to get to know my sister, as well as visit the Silver Lake area where my life took root, and look for clues that would lead me to Frank Mazzola.

The next morning I was raring to get started on my excavating mission. This time it wouldn't be long distance phone calls; I'd be on location where my history took place. A pilgrimage that would take me over the same paths my family from the "other side" had trod. Just thinking about it while I dressed that morning got my juices flowing. I was also planning a hunt, which had a hint of danger to it. Even with Rebecca's doomful warning, I had decided to seek out my natural father.

I had a quick continental breakfast with ReeAnn and Bill. They could tell my anxiety level was high, and were reminding me of particulars as though they had a check-list. I received a last minute briefing on the best routes to take to get to my various destinations. Soon I was off, traversing the freeways of Los Angeles. My first destination was Frank Mazzola's most recent business address on Pico Boulevard, which, in 1987, was a beauty supply outlet. As I drove toward Pico, I reminisced how I had obtained Mazzola's last business address.

Several weeks earlier, after finding out my natural father's name, and knowing he had been in the liquor business, I contacted the California State Liquor Licensing Agency in Sacramento to see if they had a listing of him. I had already tried the Los Angeles telephone information operators for a listing, with no success. After several calls and beaureaucratic maneuvers, I finally got through to the right office, which was located in Riverside. I talked with a gentleman who said he remembered the name Frank Mazzola. When I heard that my blood pressure rose a little. He said there had been a case involving him several years back. My excitement grew to trepidation, and I wondered what I was in for. I tried to tactfully uncover a hint of what the case involved, but he successfully sidestepped my probes. I just hoped it didn't have anything to do with mysterious disappearances.

I asked if he had Mazzola's current home address or phone number. He said he thought they had it, but only as current as 1983. He put me on hold, while he went to get the file. I was starting to taste victory—I was closing in. When he came back on, he wanted to know the reason for my request. This was starting to sound like an information operator grilling, and I had a sinking feeling that my fish just got away. I told him I was an old friend of the family's, and had lost contact twenty years back. I told him it was extremely important that I get hold of Mazzola, and that I had tried all other avenues to find him. For some reason, the man that was helping me had changed completely. His demeanor went from very accommodating to very negative, almost hostile. He either had talked with someone, or had read something. When I thought back on our conversation, there was another emotion evident in the man's voice. He was scared. The only information he'd give me was the address of Mazzola's last business establishment, which he did. He also told me Mr. Mazzola had been in the liquor business until 1983, when his liquor license expired. That was all. He said if I wanted any personal information on Mr. Mazzola, I'd have to talk to their regional director. I asked for his number and he gave it to me. I called the director's office at least six times over the next week and he was either not there or was "tied up." He never returned my calls. It was so blatant that his secretary recognized my voice before I identified myself, and would apologize and give some excuse. I was starting to get extremely aggravated, but decided it wasn't worth it. What was it that caused the man to change by a hundred-eighty degrees, and the director to neglect me? Were they afraid of something or someone?!

Armed with Frank Mazzola's last business address, I called the information operator to see if I could get a phone number. The first operator said an address wasn't enough for me to get a phone number. She didn't know who she was dealing with. I'd been up this trail several times. I asked to talk with her supervisor. She said it would make no difference, but I insisted and she reluctantly put her supervisor on the phone. The supervisor asked what the nature of my emergency was that I had to have this number. She implied that it damn near had to be a life or death situation. I started to get frustrated. I never had such a hard-nosed operator. I figured this was my best lead, and before I realized it, I blurted out that my father, Frank Mazzola, owned the business located at the address, and that I hadn't seen him in many years. Acceptance was swift! The operator said she would call and ask the party if it was okay to give me the number. She said she'd call back in fifteen minutes or so. I certainly didn't intend to get in this pickle. What if he was still at this address and the operator called him to say his son Gary was looking for him? No telling the repercussions! My pulse gained a few beats. The phone rang. It was the operator. She said that Frank Mazzola no longer had a business at this address. What relief that was! However, the owner of the current business, a beauty supply outlet, knew Frank Mazzola and told her I could call him. She gave me his number.

I called the beauty supply number. The owner answered and I identified myself as the person using operator assistance. He seemed belligerent and put-out. He also sounded Italian! He said he didn't know Frank had a son named

Gary. I told him that I told the operator that only to get the phone number. I was a good friend from many years ago. He seemed to buy that, but wouldn't give me Frank's home number or address. He said Frank Mazzola was the last person he'd ever want to upset! He offered to call Mr. Mazzola and ask him if it was okay to give me his number. I thanked him and said I'd call back in two days. I gave the name Gary Kullberg, hoping that it would ring familiar. Several days later I called. The beauty supply man had talked with Mr. Mazzola. He didn't know a Gary Kullberg or want to be bothered. There would be no phone number or address. For an instant I almost let loose that I was Mr. Mazzola's son, and would he please call again? I didn't have the nerve, however, and I didn't want to involve third parties. It was just that this guy talked with and personally knew my natural father, and yet I was still far away from contacting him.

I had no problem finding the address on Pico Boulevard. When I saw the building, which was recessed off the street, I rechecked the street number. This was it, but the building wasn't a retail establishment facility. It was a warehouse. I had pictured a retail liquor store. Maybe it had been changed since 1983. I parked and walked over to the building. It was ten o'clock Saturday morning, and I wondered if somebody might be there. I wasn't sure what I'd say, but I went up and knocked on the locked door. No one was there. The beauty supply man had already done his part, what did I expect to gain by visiting him? I guess I thought if he saw my honest face, he'd relent and sneak me Frank Mazzola's phone number. Not likely!

I had always wondered just how much resemblance there would be between Mazzola and myself. What if I was his spitting image and somebody saw me who knew him? They'd be on my trail in no time. Rebecca had said they were the kind who had no mercy!

There was an adjacent business building that ran perpendicular to the warehouse. I think it was an insurance office. There was somebody there. He came to the door and was friendly. I asked about the next door beauty supply business, and if he knew the previous proprietor. He knew the present owner, but didn't know what it had been before. He didn't know a Frank Mazzola either. He said that sometimes the beauty supply man came in on Saturdays, and that I should come back later. I thanked him and headed off for some door-to-door investigative work.

I went to six or seven liquor stores in a two-block radius. I asked if they knew a Frank Mazzola who had been in the liquor business on Pico. I also went to several nearby restaurants and asked. An absolute zero. What did I expect after almost four years of being gone from the area? There was an Italian restaurant that I hoped would open so that I could inquire. About eleven o'clock, I gave up on my canvassing, and headed over to the Berkeley Avenue area to see the old Kullberg home and Mazzola liquor store.

I parked in a shopping area and walked. ReeAnn had told me that they lived on a little narrow street, almost like an alley. After looking around, I found it. I walked up the street, and the house was still there at 2017 1/2 Berkeley Avenue—the same address that was given in the *Los Angeles Times'* article about the lady who broke into Joan Crawford's home. As I stood there staring at this little house, I felt a little queasy, knowing this place was once my home. It had been my purgatory. I saw the porch where I had been kept while the Kullbergs ate their meals. I wondered in which room Kullberg had literally tossed me into my new life. Whatever happened there was gone from my memory. Any hold this house had on me was gone. My parent's love healed all those hurts, thank God. I walked down to where the liquor store had been. The building was still there, and it was a small convenience store now.

I went in and looked around. It had seen many years. This was the place where Rebecca had met and invited Frank to be her lover, resulting in my birth; where Andy and ReeAnn had bought ice cream and Andrew Kullberg bought his whiskey. Rebecca had come by here on her way to the trolley car that took her uptown and to the market to buy groceries. This place had been the crossroad for the events that led to my existence.

A *deja vu* experience happened when I was driving over to the Berkeley Avenue house area. Several blocks away there was a small, picturesque lake. The boulevard off the freeway followed the shoreline for a quarter mile or so. The lake was immediately familiar to me. I remember coming by that lake many times with my parents when we came to downtown Los Angeles to shop. That particular part of the shopping trip was always my favorite spot. ReeAnn told me Rebecca would take us kids over to the lake on sunny days. Those were probably the happiest days back then. Now I understood the emotional feelings I had for that lake when my parents and I unwittingly drove by.

After sightseeing and a little detective work, I had a bite of lunch near the Berkeley Avenue house. From the little cafe, I had an excellent view of the old liquor store, and I started thinking about Frank Mazzola. I knew he had a brother, Paul; had been in business only three years ago; was approximately seventy-one years old; was easily contacted by the beauty supply man, which meant he probably was in the Los Angeles area; and probably had an unlisted phone number.

I decided to try the Pico address one more time, and if the beauty supply man wasn't there, I'd find a pay phone and get acquainted with the Los Angeles information operator for unlisted numbers. During the twenty minute drive over, I formulated a plan in case the man who knew Frank Mazzola was there. When he came to the door, I'd introduce myself as Gary Kullberg, the person who had called from Dallas, Texas several weeks earlier, regarding the whereabouts of Frank Mazzola. I couldn't use my name, for fear he'd remember the one I'd given him on the phone. I'd explain that it was very important for me to contact Frank, as I had sensitive, confidential information to pass on to his brother Paul. If he knew Frank as well as I thought, using Paul's name might give me the credibility I needed, as well as the fact that I was here from Texas. Hopefully, I'd convince him to call Frank and then let me talk to him in private. My delivery had to be in such a way he couldn't take the chance of refusing me. That sounded like a good plan. There didn't seem to be any negatives, except if he asked to see identification, which was unlikely. If he asked, I'd say I didn't have any with me. There was one thing I needed to remember—to mentally note an escape route. I went over the simple plan several times, and was set to make my move. Planning that visit was not unlike the thought process in a chess game, which involved visualizing moves and counter moves.

Just a few blocks to go. I thought, even if the beauty supply man wasn't there, this plan might work by long distance. However, the timing wouldn't be as effective as playing it out in person. I was getting close to the warehouse, which was just around the next corner. I turned into the parking area, which had no cars. I knocked on the door quite a few times and finally gave up. Damn! I'd have to put that plan away for possible future activation. Down the street from the warehouse was a gas station and several phone booths, and that's where I headed.

I called information and went through the usual hassle of getting the supervisor who handled unlisted numbers. I asked if it was possible to have the entire Los Angeles area checked for an unlisted number, and she said, "Yes, but you'll be charged $3.50." I agreed, but didn't have the change, so asked that it be charged to my home phone number. I gave her the name, Frank Mazzola, and told her that there was a personal family emergency and it was necessary that I contact him. The operator agreed, and called my home in Texas to verify that the charge would be accepted. My wife okay'd the request, but wondered what in the world I was up to. She wasn't worried, just curious, as I had done this before. The operator got back on the line, and told me it would take thirty to forty-five minutes and to stay by the phone. After about thirty-five minutes, the phone rang, and the operator confirmed there was no

173

unlisted number for a Frank Mazzola in the Los Angeles area. That meant he must have a listed number. I asked at the service station for directions to the nearest library. The man said there was a small branch library just four blocks away. As I pulled up in front of the building, I remember thinking this was the smallest library facility I'd ever seen, and figured I'd eventually have to find a larger one. It was a cozy little place with the usual circular tables, and was cramped with book racks. I walked up to the front desk and asked if I could see all their telephone directories. I planned to systematically check out every city directory in the Los Angeles area, and eventually southern California if necessary. This branch had about ten, which was more than I expected. I took several volumes over to a table. The first book was large and included about eight incorporated areas. I expected to be there for some time, but a miracle happened. About the sixth city in the first book gave me a listing for Frank Mazzola. I couldn't believe my eyes! I copied the phone number and address, and headed for my rental car.

I needed time to plan my next move. I was at a crucial point in this chess game. It was about one o'clock in the afternoon, so I had plenty of time. Why not go over to San Fernando Valley and check out the address? That seemed like a good passive plan. I just wasn't ready to make a phone call right then. I wanted to see where Frank Mazzola lived and then I'd call him.

It took about a half hour to get to San Fernando Valley from Los Angeles proper. Then I needed to find a place called Mission Hills, which, according to my map, was in the middle of the valley. Mission Hills wasn't a very big area, so my job would be easy to find the street and number. Wrong! I literally spent hours looking for the street, Woodle Avenue. I went to three different service stations, searching their maps for Woodle Avenue. It didn't exist. I rechecked the local telephone directory, and Frank Mazzola was listed at 10536 Woodle Avenue, Mission Hills. I called information and it was a good, current listing, according to the operator. Where the hell was Woodle Avenue? I went to the Mission Hills Fire Station, thinking they would surely know. It wasn't on their map either! The closest thing to Woodle was Woodley. That was the answer—the "y" had been dropped off. I went up and down Woodley. There was no 10536. That number didn't exist. I found where it might be, and asked, with negative results. Then I went to the main post office, and asked if Woodley or Woodle was right for Mazzola. They didn't know either. I was beside myself with frustration. At both the fire station and the post office, I pointed to the phone directory, which had been verified by AT&T. All I got were puzzled looks. Of course, the obvious question they all asked me was, "Why don't you call the party and find out where they live?" A good question! That's just what I ended up doing. When I called, I got a recording that said Frank Mazzola wasn't available and to leave a message. I hung up and decided to call again from Texas. I left Mission Hills shaking my head. What was happening? Was this a "front" operation or what? I just didn't know what to think.

It was a good forty-minute drive back to ReeAnn's place. The Woodle address mystery prompted me to think about Frank Mazzola and his background. Besides a few personal facts I knew from Rebecca and the Children's Home bio sketch, I had read a few books on Sicily and the Sicilian Mafia. When I first thought about Sicily, a scene came to mind—probably from the movie, *The Godfather.* I pictured a small rural village near Palermo, sweltering in the mid-afternoon heat. Dust whisked off a dirt road near a house with chickens and dogs scurrying about in the yard. The inhabitants were packed in the house trying to keep cool with drinks, while others were taking an afternoon siesta. Dark sweat stains showed on the clothing of submachine gun-toting bodyguards, stationed under several olive trees around the house.

I had always thought of Sicily as an island historically belonging to Italy, where Mafia members originated. Its rich heritage had somehow escaped me in my history classes. Sicilians are a hybrid unto themselves, with the blood of Sicani (Stone Age), Greeks, Carthaginians, French, Germans, Spanish and Romans flowing through their veins. Their roots reach back to the beginning of mankind. I wondered where the Mazzola heritage fit in the scheme of Sicily's history.

Rebecca mentioned that the Mazzolas had immigrated to this country from Palermo, Sicily in 1921, when Frank was five. Palermo was not only the capitol of Sicily, but the power center for the Mafia. Several times, in recent history, the Italian government has attempted to eliminate the Sicilian Mafia. Most notably when Benito Mussolini's Fascist regime came into power after 1922, when many of the Mafia leaders (approximately 150), were captured and brought to trial. It was during the early 1920's that there was a large migration of Sicilians to the United States and South America to escape the purge. The Mazzola family evaded the liquidation and came to the United States. When Rebecca Kullberg knew Frank Mazzola in the late 1930's and early 1940's, the family had a well-established liquor business, with six or seven stores throughout the Los Angeles area. She remembered Frank telling her his family had been in the wine and liquor business for generations. So, it wasn't difficult to conjecture the business that Guissepe Mazzola pursued in his new homeland in 1922.

I searched for subject matter about the Mafia and bootlegging in California or Los Angeles, and found only an occasional geographic reference to them, with no names or specifics. Very few western U.S. cities had big time Mafia operations fifty to sixty years ago. All the major Mafia families were in the midwest or east. Of the many Mafia names I ran across in my research, there wasn't one Mazzola. However, I did run across an author by the name of Reparata Mazzola, who coauthored, with Sonny Gibson, a nonfiction biography entitled, *Mafia Kingpin*.

Organized crime in the United States has been likened to the Sicilian Mafia in its philosophy, methods of operations and local organization. During the 1950's and '60's, Mafia operations were conducted by twenty–four individual groups or "families" scattered throughout the United States. There were several large scale investigations by the Congress and Presidential Commission, that tried to prove the existence of a Sicilian Mafia national leadership, and that there was a direct tie-in with Palermo, Sicily. Neither case was substantiated. By the 1970's, the U.S. Sicilian Mafia seemed to be gradually changing with the disappearance of old-style bosses. The "operations" have become much more sophisticated and subtle in action. However, the Sicilian soul of the organization is still there, embodied in such qualities, as: respect and honor, promises kept at any cost, code of silence, cold-bloodedness, instilled fear and terror, and vengeance! It was that last quality that played on my mind. Several of the books repeated that theme. Sicilians had a reputation for being far from the easiest people to govern, and were characterized as the most vengeful and passionate people in the world!

I spent that evening visiting with ReeAnn and Bill, and took them to dinner. I bid farewell the next morning and left for the Los Angeles International Airport. After several days back home in Texas, I dialed the number for the Frank Mazzola residence in Mission Hills, California.

The phone rang several times. There wasn't going to be a recording this time. A young lady answered. I asked if this was the Frank Mazzola residence. The answer was yes—he was her husband. I inquired if he had been in the liquor business. She said it sounded like I was looking for her husband's uncle. I asked if she knew how I could contact his uncle, who was an old friend that I hadn't seen in years. The last she knew, he was living in Beverly Hills, but said he moved quite often, and was hard to keep track of. When she told me that, there was a change in her tone—it was a menacing quality. Especially when she said, "Good luck, you'll need it!" I wasn't sure whether she meant I'd need luck to find him or . . . afterwards. It occurred to me that this was Frank's brother, Paul's son's family. I asked if

177

I could have her father-in-law, Paul's phone number. She said, "Sure," and gave it to me. I was getting close. When I thanked her and said good-bye, I should have asked about the address enigma, but didn't.

I remembered Rebecca telling me that Paul was at the liquor store when she brought me over to show Frank. I was sure he knew of my existence. If, and when, I called Paul, I realized events might have a force all their own, much as they did when I first called Andy Kullberg. This time my life could literally hang in the balance. What if I was intruding on sacred Sicilian family grounds? A family that had Mafia ties, the Mazzolas, might consider me a threat to have around. What a chess game this was turning into!

I called Paul Mazzola. I gave him my name, and told him I was trying to get in touch with his brother, Frank, who I'd known many years ago. Paul sounded very Italian. I could almost see his hand gestures. He wasn't buying my story. He wanted to know who I was and how I knew Frank. When I sidestepped his questions, I sensed he was getting agitated. He wasn't about to give me a hint about Frank. In fact, his patience seemed near exhaustion. I decided truth was my only ally.

I told Paul that what I was about to tell him was very personal, and I'd make it as short as possible. I started out by saying I was born June 3, 1941, and forty-four years ago I was adopted. Before I could get another word out, Paul stopped me and said his brother lived in Palm Springs, and gave me his phone number. I thanked him and our conversation ended. Paul didn't want to get involved in his brother's business. He knew who I was!

It took me a day to build the courage to call my natural father. I figured if I procrastinated much longer, they'd figure out where I lived. Paul had probably alerted the "family" and I needed to tell my side of the story before anything happened. My mind replayed bits and parts of *The Godfather.* I dialed the number. The phone rang somewhere in Palm Springs. Frank Mazzola finally answered. I gave him my name. When he spoke, it sounded like I was interrupting his dinner. He was eating something. I offered to call back in half an hour. He said, "Yea, sure." That's all I needed! That half hour was an eternity. I waited thirty-five minutes and called again, and he answered.

He sounded much like his brother, with a melodic, Southern Italian resonance. His impatience was immediately evident. His tone demanded what it was that I wanted. I gave him my name and told him I thought we might be related. I told him my story was personal, and I needed to know if he was the right Frank Mazzola. Would he tell me the street his liquor store was on in the early 1940's? He immediately gave the answer. He was the one.

I told him my story as briefly as I could, concluding with my natural mother giving the name Frank Mazzola as my natural father. I asked him if he understood what I was saying. He said he understood, and admitted that he was the one I was looking for. I told him that if he wished, I would hang up the phone, and he would never hear from me again, that I didn't want to interfere with his family. He said he definitely wanted to see me! I could hear someone in the background, probably family members. He said he had two children, who now have their own families. I told him I would be in California in several weeks, and maybe we could visit. He said he'd like that.

It was early November 1986, when I had initially talked with Frank Mazzola. Sue and Mike were both out for the evening, and I had the house to myself, which was good. Consummate privacy was necessary for me to conduct such a personal affair as communicating with my natural father for the first time in my life. I had listened for any utterance or intonation that would give me clues to the nature of his being. After my call, I reflected on my impressions of Frank Mazzola. At first he seemed very impatient, almost rude, but then I'm not unlike that when hearing an unfamiliar voice, which often foretells of a salesman or fundraising tirade. As I told him my story, his demeanor mellowed, and his voice took on a quality of both contemplation and astonishment. I couldn't tell if he was in awe of the history that was taking place, or calculating how to "deal" with this unfortunate development. When he said he definitely wanted to see me, what did that mean? Was it curiosity or the opportunity to personally deliver an ultimatum? I imagined at the conclusion of our coffee house visit, he might threaten, "If you ever interfere in my life again, you're a dead person!" As I thought about it, I really didn't give him much choice, but to see me. If he accepted my offer to hang up and not be heard from again, then this phantom from the past would still be free for future extortion or invasion of privacy without warning. He mentioned his family, a son and daughter, who had families of their own, and I wondered how I could possibly fit into his life. It was clear Frank Mazzola had to meet me to see and know how to rectify the situation. My initial feelings of elation were quickly assuming the face of dread. When Sue came home, I told her of the momentous call to the "other side," but omitted my fears.

Contact

Two weeks went by quickly, and before I knew it, I was in San Diego, California. This was the last stop of a three-day college recruitment trip for my company. I had very full schedules before coming to San Diego State University, but the appointment list was short there, and it looked like I would wrap up by early afternoon on Friday. I had flown in early Thursday evening, and the weather was splendid, letting me know I was back home in Southern California.

I had dinner near my motel and later strolled along the beach, which provided the chance for exercise and quiet contemplation. I was thinking about tomorrow's visit with Frank. My imagination had played out that encounter many times during the last several weeks. I'm not often taken to nocturnal dreaming, but that was the case two or three nights running. The setting was in the living room of a house, and a shadowy figure of a man was studying me. Soon, a feminine figure came in through sliding glass doors and a horrible argument ensued over my existence. About that time I would awake in a cold sweat. The implication was obvious. I didn't tell Susan, as I didn't want her to worry about my state of mind, and besides, I was sure that everything would turn out okay. It was a case of subconscious accommodation to the bizarre discoveries in my life.

I headed back toward my motel as I wanted to get to bed early. I had a full slate of morning interviews, starting at eight o'clock. When I crossed the street, I noticed two swarthy men looking my way from the motel entrance. My heart skipped a beat. I continued onward, knowing my mind was tired and prone to exaggeration at that point. Once back in my room, I remembered my promise to call

Frank Mazzola so that we could arrange a meeting time and place in Palm Springs.

I called Frank and told him I'd be in Palm Springs about four o'clock in the afternoon the next day. He seemed as excited as I was. He said to call him when I arrived, and we'd meet at a restaurant for coffee and a visit. He casually asked if I had a rental car and I said yes. He didn't suggest meeting at his home. What did I expect? His wife probably wouldn't be interested in meeting me—or, blood on the carpet would be incriminating.

I must say, all things considered, the anticipation of meeting him was great. At the same time, I couldn't help wondering if there would be some kind of Machiavellian surprise waiting for me. A one-way trip into the California desert? I remembered Rebecca's ominous warning about the Mafia connection and mysterious disappearances. Events were lining up too easily.

The next morning was foggy and cool. I found my way to the placement center with no problem, and began my interviews. The morning went fast, and before I knew it, my last appointment was finished and the sun was out. I drove back to the motel to freshen up and change into more comfortable clothes, and picked up the personal packet of papers and photos I had prepared to share with Mazzola. As I drove out, I stopped at the office to verify that my Palm Springs route was the most efficient. To get to Palm Springs from San Diego, it was necessary to go north on Interstate 15, and at Riverside take Highway 60 East which merged with Interstate 10 East, going on to the Springs. It was necessary to travel the two legs of the triangle, because high mountains blocked the hypotenuse.

The drive from San Diego to Palm Springs takes two and a half to three hours. I remember the trip like it was yesterday. My concentration was at peak performance, much as it was during a tournament chess match. Some games I can remember for years. The weather was clear, with a slight breeze. I stopped in Riverside for gas and a stretch. The closer I got to Palm Springs, the more I would

182

catch myself checking to see if I was being followed. I remembered that he had asked about my transportation—Rent-A-Car? I couldn't remember if I gave him the rental company's name. I thought maybe—would they trace me? I even told him my route. My mind was playing tricks on me—or was it?

About fifteen miles from the Springs, a strange sight appeared in the distance. There were thousands of sticks that seemed to dance and glisten in the dusk sunlight. As I came closer, I realized they were windmills, thousands of them! I'd never seen so many in all my life. What a welcome at the end of my journey. I tried to remember who wrote about *Windmills of the Mind*. Mine was starting to spin.

I was getting close now. I took the turn off from Highway 10 toward Palm Springs. It looked the same as it had the last time I was at this beautiful desert oasis. That was twenty-six years ago. Palm Springs was bound to have changed, but the majestic mountains that rose from the desert floor, shielding the estates of the rich and famous, were still familiar. I had come to the Springs at the invitation of a fraternity brother over spring break in 1960. What fun times we had! The place was packed with young college people. I remembered cruising the main drag with my fraternity brothers, looking for coeds and parties. My frat brother's family had a super home, with a pool and tennis courts. There were about ten of us staying at his place. That was a long time ago.

As I approached the city, it was almost unfamiliar because of all the new building developments. I recognized Bob Hope's fabulous dome-shaped palace, high on the hill overlooking Palm Springs. I had seen pictures of it in a magazine, and to see it, even at a distance, made it believable. The lush green of the lawns and beautiful landscaped homes were in outstanding contrast with the stark desert surroundings.

I pulled into a service station. It was windy, but warm for a fall November day. After freshening up, I studied the big city map. I was about thirty minutes early, so I thought I'd sneak a look at Frank's place before I called, since I wouldn't have the chance afterward. I finally found his street on the map. He lived in a community development, and getting to his place wasn't going to be easy, as the maze of streets meandered without a set pattern. It looked like they followed golf course fairways, which ran irregularly throughout the residential area. It took me twenty minutes to drive to the general area. The curving avenues, which started and ended to accommodate the plush golf links, prompted me to buy a local map. I located his short street, and proceeded to follow the many turns and jaunts ever so slowly. My heart was pounding so fast and hard, I swear my whole body started to shake! One more turn and I would be on his street! I could feel the sweat on my brow and my palms were dripping with perspiration. I turned, and there it was, the second house on the left. I went by it slowly, but tried not to stare for fear of being obvious. What if the Mazzolas came outside and noticed my interest? It was not only fear, but guilt that I was being somewhat underhanded by conducting this unauthorized personal scrutiny of the Mazzola home. I went up the street and turned around, coming by a second time. No one seemed to notice me and my mind had captured the picture. It was a nice cozy place, landscaped with desert fauna and had a carport, which housed his car and golf cart. As I accelerated back toward Palm Springs proper, I started looking for another service station with a pay phone. I called Frank and he directed me to a service station right near his home, which I remembered going by. He said he'd meet me there in ten or fifteen minutes.

I arrived at the Standard Station before Frank. It was a large facility and crowded. I parked and waited. After about ten minutes, I got out of the car to stretch and look around. My concentration was keen. I was mentally cataloging every vehicle and their occupants, and the inventory must have approached twenty automobiles at the peak of activity. My mission was not unlike that of a Secret Service Agent securing an area to insure his ward's safety. Finally, I recognized his car on the far side of the service station, moving slowly, and a silver-haired, dark-complected gentleman scanning the lot. He seemed to be by himself. I waved and he drove over. He stopped by me and asked if I was Gary. We shook hands through his car window.

There was no doubt in my mind; the instant I shook his hand and saw him, that this was my natural father. All fear of anything happening to me evaporated. I could tell he felt the same communion. The melodic sound of his Italian voice was mesmerizing and beckoning to me. He wanted me to follow him home. That was a surprise. I didn't know what to expect next. I followed and in five minutes, I was pulling in behind him in his driveway. I got out and walked over to him. He opened his arms and gave me a big hug and welcomed me home!

My relief was indescribable. The tension that had built up from my fears and anxieties was gone. The unwinding was aided by a cool goblet of fine white wine! The toasts were as frequent as the refills. Salute!

We had a nice long visit. He was living by himself. His wife passed away eight years ago. He said he'd always wondered about me. He had married an Italian girl—somewhat arranged by his family—in 1947. Ironically, she could not have children. They went to all kinds of doctors. They ended up adopting a boy and a girl.

He had always wanted to find me, since I was his only biological offspring. As he told me his story, tears came to his eyes. He said he hadn't seen Rebecca or me since that fateful time she brought me to his liquor store, and had no idea how to search for me. He had thought of pursuing the Crawford connection, but never got around to it. Now all that was important was the chance to get to know each other. He took me to a fine Italian Restaurant and the evening was enjoyable.

As we drove through Palm Springs to the restaurant, Frank took me by several estates of the famous who reside there. Among them being Jerry Ford, Malcolm Baldridge and Frank Sinatra. The latter he counts as a friend whom he sees occasionally. He fondly talks of his friend, Tommy LaSorda, who gets him tickets to Dodger games. When we drove up to the restaurant, the valet opened Frank's door and said, "Good evening, Mr. Mazzola." We were greeted inside by the maitre d' with an equally familiar welcome, and so went the evening. We were truly given first-class treatment. The waiter was at our beck and call, taking pictures, etc., and would have done cartwheels, if Frank had asked him.

Frank gave me a brief rundown of his life over dinner. His family came from Palermo, Sicily, in 1921, when he was five years old. Paul, his brother, was eight. He always liked math subjects in school. I understood.

He had played football in high school. When the war started, he went into the army. He was an artillery-man. His knee had been injured in a freak artillery shell explosion. Shrapnel hit his legs. When his company commander found out Frank's background, he became the head bartender at the Officer's Club. Frank said they were always asking him to line up extra "Special Provisions." Later in the war, he was an interpreter for the Italian POW's brought to the States.

I could see the similarities in the two of us. We have similar head shapes, especially from the nose up. He's just under six feet tall, has silver hair, which he says was black as a young man. his eyes are agate-colored. Around the iris is a blue ring with brown interior. He said his father had blue eyes and his mother, brown. His father's blue eyes must have been the Norman influence. Like me, he says he's never had a cavity.

Frank has an impatience about him that I can identify with. He also communicates with his hands by gesture and touch, just as I do. He is much more extroverted than me. He's the "life of the party" type. He has been on many world cruises in recent years and really enjoys them. In fact, he was leaving for a month's trip to the South Pacific after my visit.

Even though Rebecca had put the fear of God into me about the Mazzola family, she also gave me a tender, personal insight of Frank. She never accused him of pursuing her; in fact, she admits it was all her doing. Rebecca says Frank was very much a gentleman, and it was obvious he had a good family upbringing. He was polite, chivalrous and showed respect. He had been taught all the personal virtues of the old country. She says the Mazzolas were a very religious family, and that Frank's mother thought he should go into the priesthood. All in all, she says Frank was a good person. She also said, with a smile, he was bashful and a good lover. Frank once told me, "Yes, our affair lasted awhile, but we were always discreet." His comment was in rebuttal to ReeAnn's "love in the country" story, which he doesn't remember.

The Mazzola family vineyards were situated in a mountainous area about thirty miles southeast of Palermo, near a little village called San Guiseppe. Frank's mother's people originally came from Palermo, and the marriage was arranged by the two families, who had long-time close ties.

When it was decided to immigrate to the United States, his dad came to New York a year before the family to establish his business. Over a year later, his dad sent for them and they came by steamer. Frank remembers that his mother had a hard time of it with two young sons because of the long confining voyage and sea sickness. He says New York was a tough place to live back in those days, and that young immigrants soon learned the real estate "turf" boundaries. "Turfs" were controlled by various neighborhood gangs that pretty much followed their national origins. They weren't there a year when they moved to the Silver Lake area of Los Angeles, California. Frank told me their new life on the West Coast was much better than New York, as they loved the more moderate climate, slower lifestyle and open space. In fact, Southern California was much more like their native Sicily.

Frank said his dad personally knew Al Capone and other Mafia figures. His family had always been in the wine and liquor business, and during prohibition, the Mafia connection helped. He said his family had the facilities to mass produce liquor during that time. In the Mojave Desert area they had several acres of underground stills. They were suitably camouflaged by canopies, making detection next to impossible. He said they had four or five large sedans for bringing the booze to Los Angeles. The springs on the vehicles had been replaced with special heavy-duty springs so that the weight wouldn't show. The Mazzola liquor/wine enterprise was a major producer for the Los Angeles area. The Feds were paid well for their cooperation. His dad had close to three hundred wine outlets in neighborhoods throughout Los Angeles. I asked him if there were ever "family" wars, and he looked at me and said, "If somebody steals your business, what can you do?"

As we talked about the bootlegging days, Frank smiled and related an incident that happened when he was fifteen. He said his dad and uncle worked out a unique method of making booze deliveries. His uncle owned and operated a bakery at the time, and the process involved hollowing out loaves of bread to accommodate small pint-size bottles of Gordon Gin. They carefully inserted the illegal product in the heart of loaves, and made deliveries in this fashion for almost a year. The Feds became wise to the scheme, and raided his uncle's establishment, temporarily putting him out of business. The affair made the Los Angeles newspapers, and Frank's friends teased him about it for years, asking when they were going to get their loaf of bread.

Earlier in the evening, Frank had mentioned that his stepfather had passed away six months after his mother had died, but never said what happened to his dad. After the account of the bakery incident, I asked him, and he said, "Gary, I think you should know about your grandfather." He gave me a grim stare, and proceeded to tell me an incredible story.

In 1931 his dad was involved in power struggles that were life-threatening and his family feared for his well-being. He was a ruthless, severe man, and had upset other "business interests" in the Los Angeles area to the point that he had to abruptly leave California for New York. Frank says his dad gathered the family, and told them he was going to New York to re-establish himself there, and would send for them in a year or so. He remembers it well, as his mother was crying, while his dad was trying to tell him and his brother what needed to be done. His dad called once a month and wrote often for about a year. Then suddenly, nothing! He simply ceased to exist! Family members in the New York area tried to find out what happened to him, but they never found a trace. His family suspected he was the target of an underworld "contract." They contacted family in Palermo to search from that end, but to no avail. No one has ever heard from, or knows what fate befell him. Of course, there was talk of revenge, but they never knew for sure who put the wheels in motion. Frank's mother was beside herself with grief, and waited ten years before remarrying. Frank tells that those were frightening and sad times for them. I sensed he didn't want to discuss the subject any further, and so I didn't pursue it. The reality that my natural grandfather met such an end was troublesome, to say the least. His life had been truly like a chess game, but for keeps!

After Frank Mazzola retired, Mazzola Wine sales have been decreasing. He relived some of the Mazzola Wine history with me and told me the story about trying to get the Mazzola Wine label. The U.S. Patent Office insisted that the Mazola (with one z) "corn oil" people approve the label, since the names were so similar. Frank said the "corn oil" people had loved the wine and there had been no problem. Sales were good and he had several large accounts, such as Howard Johnson's. Then came the end of "Fair Trade" and the "little man" was pushed out by big companies like Gallo and other mass producers. When I left Frank's home, he gave me two gallons of Mazzola Wine to take with me, and I found it to be delicious, outstanding wine!

As I drove back to San Diego that night, my mind was reveling at all the new discoveries in my life. The next morning I was flying up North to visit my dad over the weekend. The question was whether I should tell Dad my story? I knew he'd find it interesting, but was afraid the interest might turn into hurt and distrust. I didn't want anything to come between us. I needed more time, so I decided not to tell Dad at that time. I knew, though, that I was putting off the inevitable. My story was one that would travel fast, especially in my hometown, and I wanted to be the one to tell Dad.

I didn't get back to my motel room much before two o'clock that morning in San Diego. Frank had tried to talk me into spending the night at his place, but I begged off because of my flight late the next morning. He wanted me to not only stay the night, but postpone my flight back to Dallas, and visit with him a day or two. I thanked him for the invitation and told him I had engagements back home and needed to get back. I didn't tell him of my weekend visit with Dad and let him think I was going back to Texas. His insistence that I stay the weekend in Palm Springs prompted my silent deceit as I didn't want to get into a discussion about *where* I should spend my time. The juggling act had begun! I wondered how long I could keep up this duplicitous relationship without hurting either of them.

I soon found that at times the pressure on me was almost unbearable, but to them I had to keep both ends of the candle lit.

The wake-up call came all too soon, but I had much packing to do before heading off for my eleven o'clock flight that morning. I had papers strewn all over the room, from recruitment interviews to notes on Frank Mazzola. On the way to the San Diego Airport, I found a place to pack the wine and caught my flight in the nick of time. At the other end, Dad was waiting there to help me.

Dad helped me with my luggage and gave me the car keys for the short drive home. He was bubbling over with news about the hometown folks I knew, and he had a full weekend planned for us. I tried to act as natural as possible.

190

I never imagined how difficult it would be. The ache within me was testament to my betrayal, but I had to keep my wits about me and act as though nothing had changed, when in fact, my world was upside down! At home I opened the car trunk and selected the luggage I'd need for the weekend. Dad noticed the carton containing two gallons of Mazzola Wine. He asked me about them, and I casually lied, "Oh, a friend asked me to bring them back for him—it's a special wine label he likes."

Dad seemed to be satisfied with my reply and no more was said. Thank God the cocktail hour arrived soon. That time of day is always a relaxing and enjoyable occasion at Dad's. Several friends usually come over, especially when I'm in town, and this time was no exception. After several Scotches, my mental equilibrium was stabilized, and I was over my crisis. I told them all about my college recruiting activities, and talked about Sue and our sons. Then, after dinner, I excused myself and went to bed early, blaming it on an unusually busy trip. As I bid good night, I told Dad to be sure and rouse me for our traditional early morning walk.

Unfortunatley, I don't get home near as much as I'd like or should, and on an average see Dad two times a year. I've tried to get him to come visit us in Texas, but his wife hates and refuses to fly, and he's reluctant to come without her. Also, for those in their mid-eighties, travel becomes more difficult. Often when I come home to visit, my stepsister and her husband would fortuitously drop in with a fully prepared meal, which is always excellent—especially her enchiladas. They are super fun people and take good care of the folks. I've always tried to plan a visit to coincide with my high school reunions, but so far have been unsuccessful. Hopefully, I'll make the thirty-year reunion in 1989.

At precisely seven, fifteen in the morning, Dad woke me up to join him on his daily two-mile walk. He rarely misses a day, and one could set a clock by his coming and going. At eighty-six, Dad is in excellent physical condition and mentally keen. I love those walks with Dad. We talk

191

about old and new times and almost always run into others we know who are out for their early morning strolls. If Dad sees somebody he thinks I haven't met, there's no hesitation to initiate introductions. In fact he loves it. I'm sure I've met everyone in his neighborhood at least three times.

During the course of our walk we go from one end of the development to the other, which takes us by the par-three golf course, clubhouse, and swimming pool. Most residences in this retirement community are duplexes and are dutifully maintained through the association. All exterior landscaping is impeccably manicured and alive with colorful flowers and a variety of trees and shrubs. In the twenty years they have lived there, it still looks the same. That constancy appeals to my traditional and conservative nature. The only thing that changes is the people, who of course, get older and occasionally make the transition to the next life.

Dad and I move along at a good pace and are back at the house in thirty-five-to-forty minutes, depending on the number of visits along the way.

After a multi-coursed breakfast, we spend lazy mornings perusing *The Los Angeles Times* and other local newspapers, and occasionally accomplish a chore or two. Sometimes we go downtown and drop in on old friends, and Dad especially enjoys calling on associates at the bank where he spent a good part of his life. Invariably, I get the urge to go by our old home and relive memories. The appearance and fabric of the neighborhood have changed considerably, but the feelings and ghosts of the past are still there.

When I drive over to my old neighborhood by myself, I'll often park and slowly walk up and down our block. Like magic, flashes of memory take me back to my childhood . . . hitting baseballs in the street, playing hide-and-seek, tossing footballs, flying kites, and mowing lawns. I can see so many things as though they happened only a short time ago. I see my childhood friends frolicking in their yards and hear their joyous shouts and laughter. I have to take a deep breath to keep from becoming too emotional. What potent stuff memories are!

After lunch, Dad and I go play pitch and putt golf on their par-three community course several blocks away. If it's warm, I'll go for a swim and lounge poolside, chatting with Dad. By then it's almost time to gather again for libations and social intercourse with friends.

On Sunday we go to All Saints Episcopal Church where, even though the santuary has been rebuilt since my childhood, the hallowed ground there magically brings back memories of days gone by . . . the happy times of Christmas and Easter . . . and the time of sorrow when I bid farewell to my mother. That Sunday after Palm Springs, I prayed to God for wisdom and guidance in my changed and complicated life. During the service my dad put his hand on my shoulder, as if he knew something was weighing heavily on my soul. It was all I could do to keep my composure.

That afternoon I bid Dad and his loving wife, farewell, and flew home to Dallas.

Loose Ends

As I write this, it has been almost two years since my first contact with the other side. It has been a fascinating journey. From the moment I first talked to Andy Kullberg in late April, 1986, I had one consuming desire—to unravel the secrets of my life. I would not be denied. As I bring this odyssey to a close, there are a few loose ends.

In May 1987, I flew to San Francisco for my son David's graduation from the University of California at Berkeley. Dave was getting his degree in Engineering Physics. My son John and I witnessed the proud moment.

It was a beautiful spring day, and the pomp and circumstance—together with the spectacular setting in the Greek Theatre—was a perfect culmination of his four years at Berkeley.

Another distant relative was getting his degree at the same exercise. He was a nephew by marriage of a second cousin of mine who lives in Sacramento. My cousin's name is George Deatherage. We were their guests at a fabulous post-graduation party of all the families at Creme de la Creme in Berkeley.

George and his family have always been favorite and special people of mine. When George was a young boy, he lived with my mom and dad for a short time before I came along. When I went to school in Oregon, I often stayed overnight at his home in Sacramento, to break up the long commute from Southern California. It was a favorite respite, and I looked forward to being with them.

When I first made contact with my natural mother, Rebecca, who lives close to Sacramento, I was afraid that she might do something weird. I feared she might contact the Deatherages, much as I had contacted the Kullbergs. I worried about that for some time, and I didn't want George and his family to be caught unaware. My folks were far enough away that the probability was remote she would contact them. I called and told them my story. I explained that Rebecca lived close by, and just might call. They understood and said they'd be on guard. Not long after I told them, they visited us in Texas for a few days. They were fascinated with my story. George seemed genuinely concerned with my ability to cope with these new surrealistic life discoveries. I tried to convince him, as well as myself, that I'd be alright.

While in California, I took the opportunity to visit Rebecca Kullberg and Frank Mazzola. I called Rebecca before I made the hour and a half drive from the Bay area to Sacramento. A recording stated that her phone number was no longer in service. My initial thought was that she'd moved, but the operator confirmed that only the phone number had changed. I called and Rebecca answered. It was a warm spring day, and we agreed to meet at a picnic table situated in a little grassy area behind her hotel. As I drove up, I saw her sitting at a table with three others. When I came up to the table, they stayed awhile, and then left, one by one. I didn't ask, but I think they were friends of Rebecca's, who were checking me out.

This time I could see her much better than when we visited in the hotel lobby, and she didn't seem as intimidating. Her eyes were different. The first time they were dark and menacing. In the afternoon sun her eyes were a pretty soft blue. I asked her about her phone number change, and she said it was necessary because of many harassing phone calls, day and night. Evidently some school kids discovered her claim to be Elvis Presley's mother, and had been calling her . . . chiding her.

She casually mentioned that she wanted to lose weight. I told her she ought to, for health's sake. She must weigh nearly three hundred pounds. Her voice rose a little. She proceeded to tell me her weight problem started when she gave birth to me. I asked how that was, since she had children before and after me. I soon wished I had never pursued this subject. Her soft blue eyes hardened. She said, "Well, you know Gary, I tried everything I could to abort you!" My stomach almost immediately became knotted and nauseated. "My pharmacist had given me internal solutions to break you loose and clear you from my body."

I asked, "Did I hear you say you wanted to abort me?"

She looked at me and said, "Of course," and proceeded to knock me flat. It was as if she delighted in the sting of her words. She was going for the jugular and continued, "I had not exactly wanted you, as I knew your father was Sicilian Italian and dark, and my husband was a blonde Swede. There was no way of fooling anybody. So I went over to Tarlow's Drug Store and asked the pharmacist, who was a friend, to give me something to abort you. He gave me canned ether to take in a douche. The first can did nothing. I went back and got a second can. I had one horrible, horrible pain that didn't last very long. Still, nothing happened. I went back to the druggist and he said he didn't dare give me more, it might kill me. When you were born, the ether

195

had hardened the birth passage to the point that I was ruptured, which has caused my obesity. Gary, it was truly a miracle that you were born."

Hearing her graphic account of the "ether-douche" technique, contrived to scrap my fetal beginnings was sickening. I felt unclean, as though, somehow the ether had oozed into the pores of my skin and was still there. The realization that I grew and was nourished in the body of this person across from me was unreal.

Then she told me about her efforts to have a miscarriage. How she had physically abused herself in an effort to damage the fetus in her body, hoping for expulsion. She had poked, gouged, hit herself and strenuously exercised to induce premature labor. As she put it, "You were a tough little bugger." I couldn't believe the candor of her tormenting words.

From the time we had our three sons, I had dreamed that my coming was not unlike their's. A time filled with expectation, wonder, tenderness, caring and love. The contrast was damning and the hurt was total. It was painfully evident that I hadn't been welcomed into this life.

I desperately needed to be far away from that place and person, but I couldn't move. Her words had taken their toll. I was weary and forlorn. How could a mother tell her child that she hadn't wanted him? That she had tried to eliminate him, to literally flush him into the sewers of Los Angeles? It took all my strength to ask, "How could you tell me that?" My inquiry evoked nothing. She sat motionless, staring down at her hands, and was silent. I was numb. After a few minutes of silence, I got up and left.

While I drove back to San Francisco, my sanity and feelings slowly returned to me. A sense of elation crept over me. Simply put, it was great to be alive. I've felt that way after attending funerals. I remember wondering what purpose God had for me. There had to be a reason for my existence.

I relived my visit with Rebecca many times that afternoon and evening. I had given myself every opportunity to know and understand her. The late afternoon revelation of her attempt to expel me into oblivion made her repulsive and any further communication that day was impossible. How could I come from such stuff? I couldn't change the facts of my birth, but it was then I knew my adopted mother was the warm and loving person who nurtured and truly gave me life. I was beginning to wish I had never found Rebecca.

It had been over twenty-two years since my beloved Mom passed away. Memories of her have recently come to me as if her spirit was trying to soothe my soul and quiet the unsettling revelations. I know now her life was devoted to my happiness. It takes so much time to bring about the wisdom to understand such things, and often it's too late to give the heartfelt appreciation. I have never been one to freely display my feelings until the last half–dozen years or so, and now I tell Dad every chance I get how much I love him.

Reminiscences of happy and loving moments with Mom have mystical healing properties for my spirit. As a young boy, after Dad heard my prayers, she would always come tuck me in bed and wish me "sweet dreams." Early Sunday mornings I would run to my parents' bedroom and climb in bed with her, so she could read me the funnies while I snuggled up against her. Also, her bed was a sanctuary when dreams weren't so sweet. She was such a gentle person, and always there to salve my hurts. Mothers have the innate ability to hear or sense their child's movements and sounds several rooms away, and Mom's sensitivity was close to being uncanny. Needless to say, I didn't get away with much, as she always knew where I was, and what I was doing anywhere in our house. It was darn near enjoyable to have a cold, with the attention I received. She made the best honey-lemon brandy concoction for coughs, and to this day, the smell of Ben–Gay brings a flood of pleasant memories. If Mom had a fault, she was a "soft–touch." I knew that if it was humanly possible, I could have most anything I wanted—I was spoiled. Mom shared my taste for hot, spicy foods, which made it tough for Dad's midwest cuisine. There was a Mexican food market downtown that had fresh enchiladas, tamales, chile rellenos and tacos to take home and put in the oven. Mom and I would go at least every two weeks and damn near buy the place out. I inherited my finicky persistence to find the perfect Christmas tree from her. Much to Dad's chagrin, Mom and I insisted on looking over almost every tree in town before selecting just the right one. Mom told me, no matter what kind of problem I had, she would always be there to help me. It was true. What devotion she had. There was never a doubt in her mind that I was her son!

In early June 1965, I flew to Indianapolis from El Paso, to attend a special Officer's Army training course at Fort Benjamin Harrison. The day I flew in we could see the "Indy 500" in progress. I had been there several days when Sue called at two o'clock in the morning on the eleventh of June to tell me Mom had died earlier that evening. That was the first time anyone close to me had died, except Grandpa, at which time I was too young to understand. That night my mind, heart and soul ached for the loss of her. Later that morning I flew to Los Angeles International Airport and Unc and Sue met me. The ride home was quiet. We drove up in front of my home, and for an instant, everything seemed the same. When I went in the house, I looked for her. It just wasn't possible that she was gone. Reality crept over me, and I had to find Dad. He was in my room, lying on my bed sobbing. When our eyes met, words can't describe my anguish. As I put my arms around him I never cried so hard in all my life. The tears burned my eyes and came in torrents. My voice called for Mom and the loss was great. I tried to control myself for Dad's sake, but I couldn't. It was hard for me to bid good-bye forever to my mother, in this life.

Several days after the funeral, I was visiting with a close nearby friend of my mother's. Sue had stayed home with Dad and I was by myself. This lady was so near and dear, she was like part of the family. Just before leaving, I told her how much I was going to miss my mother. She looked at me and said, "Well, Gary, you'll never miss her near as much as I will. It's not like you were her natural son, and you haven't seen her much since leaving home, whereas I've seen her almost every day!" I couldn't believe what she said. I thought maybe she said it because of her grief. But, still, she said it. My adoption cut straight through me! I have wondered if she ever thought how much her words hurt me. I never forgave her for that, and any close feelings I had for her died. If only she had known how much I loved my Mom and what she had meant to me, those words could never have come.

On June 3, 1987, I had my forty-sixth birthday. It was a weekday and a work day. It was not unlike any other birthday of recent years, except I had a surprise waiting for me upon my return from lunch. There was a note sitting in the middle of my desk from my secretary. It said, "Your mother called to wish you a happy birthday." Not thinking, I summoned my secretary and asked her what the note was all about. She gave me a rather incredulous look and said, "Your mother from Sacramento called and you weren't here, so I took the message." I'm sure I must have looked like I'd seen a ghost. My secretary gave me an odd look and left. It had been about two weeks since my stormy visit with her, and I never imagined this was possible. Later, I called Susan and she confirmed that Rebecca had called home first, and had said, "A mother never forgets her child's birthday."

When all is said and done, I don't know what to think or how I feel about Rebecca. Her blunt confession of my prenatal "final solution" had infuriated and hurt me. We have talked several times since my visit. During one of our conversations, she said, "Gary, I don't believe in abortion, and when I tried to abort you, I grievously sinned against God Almighty. I call abortion the murder of your own little helpless baby, which is mighty cruel and evil. Mothers murdering their own helpless infants! Deliberate murder! I have been paying for that sin all these years, and I hope God will forgive me."

Rebecca has told me many stories: how her husband, Andrew Kullberg, had slit his wrists, attempting to commit suicide; about several sordid hitchhiking trips across the United States she made with her children; and how she had led a cruel, nomadic life over the past thirty years. In conclusion, she feels she has paid for her sins, and has worn the scarlet letter long enough. It has become clear why there has been such a vast chasm between Rebecca and her children. Andy had tried to warn me from the beginning. Her children had distanced themselves to keep from being pulled into the pit of unspeakable and despicable horrors of the past. Their peace of mind and chance for a wholesome life made the separation necessary. All of Rebecca's children worry about her mental state. The fear is whether her condition can be passed on to future generations.

ReeAnn related a revealing story about her mother. In the summer of 1950, Rebecca journeyed back home to Indiana, taking ReeAnn and Andy with her. The trip was unremarkable, except for an incident that happened during their return to California. At thirteen and a half, ReeAnn was attractive and easily mistaken for a lady of seventeen. They had stopped for lunch in a small Nevada town, which she says was nothing more than a dusty wide spot in the road. While they ate, ReeAnn felt the lecherous stare of a man seated near them who was probably twice her age. After they finished lunch, Rebecca, having noticed the lustful interest in her daughter, approached the man and struck a deal with him. Outside the cafe, she pulled ReeAnn aside and told her the man liked her a lot, and asked if she would like to stay there with him. Rebecca said the stranger had money and would take good care of her. ReeAnn said she was absolutely livid with rage, and whatever love she had left for her mother, died. From that moment on, she stayed away from her mother as much as possible, and when ReeAnn left home, she shut Rebecca out of her life for over three decades.

I'm afraid my resurrection has been the cause of painful memories for my brothers and sisters. At first, I was welcomed as a long lost sheep of the family, however dark, and a celebrity of sorts. Since then, I have been a conduit of information and communication, and the chasm has narrowed. Rebecca's children have been forced to confront reality and the past again. I was the symbol, their "Little Pearl," of all that went wrong in their lives. They know I'm not the cause and have taken me into their homes. My energetic, persistent pursuit of personal information was enough to irritate anybody. When I visited, that's all we talked about.

My flight arrived on time in Ontario, California. Frank Mazzola had just had surgery on his knee and was laid up in the Loma Linda V. A. Hospital. He had arranged for his lady friend, Myrt, to meet me. I had seen pictures of her and had no problems picking her out in the crowded baggage claim area. After loading my bags in her car, we went straight to see Frank.

It was good to meet someone who knew him. I could get a different perspective. She took good care of me to boot. When we got to Frank's room, he didn't look too good, so we didn't stay long. He instructed us to go to his place and make ourselves at home.

Myrt and I talked during the one and a half hour drive to Frank's home. She was as interested in learning my background, as I was her's. She had met Frank on his recent cruise to the South Pacific, which was the one he had left on just three days after our first visit in November, 1986. He had not told her about me until quite awhile after their return. Myrt told me he was a very private person. She said Frank was definitely one to have things his way, and was a very orderly, neat and particular man.

As we approached Palm Springs, the windmills came into sight. I told Myrt of my fascination with them when I first came to see Frank. I stopped to take a photo, and she was amused that I would make the effort. When we were close to Frank's place, she gave me a tour of the area. Soon

201

we moved into Frank's home.

His home told much about him. Everything is in its place, and portrays a man who is fastidious and well–organized. Memorabilia from his days in the liquor business are evident throughout his home. Pictures of his daughter and son, and their families, are on display and plentiful in the bedrooms.

Frank has given me several pictures of himself as a boy and young man. I have a photo of him as a boy, which is the epitome of Little Lord Fauntleroy. His military picture has a remarkable likeness to my service photo. He gave me a color print of what he calls his "Mafioso" period. It was right out of the *Untouchables.* I have one of his mother and father, my grandparents.

Private time is important and necessary for Frank. I understand as I am the same way. Since he lives by himself, he is very selective and picks the occasions he wants companionship. He has been living by himself for some time, as he had even before his wife passed away. He and his wife had divorced ten years before she died of cancer. His son and daughter went with their mother, which caused hurt and alienation. Frank carries the old country custom that the man should be master of his family and home, and evidently his wife and her family tried to change that. Honor and respect are as much a part of him as his silver hair and broad smile. After he found out his wife was very sick, he joined her in the last years, and cared for her.

That evening Frank's next door neighbors invited Myrt and me over for cocktails before we went to dinner. I hadn't met them before, and was anxious to visit with them. From what Frank told me, they were the only ones that knew about me, other than Myrt. They told me Frank kept to himself, but at the same time was very outgoing when around friends. They often got together for "Happy Hour," but would worry sometimes because they wouldn't see him for a week at a time. He never imposed and was the ideal neighbor. As I was talking with Bill at one end of the room, I overheard Myrt and his wife discussing me and how much

I looked and acted like Frank. Later Myrt and I bid good-bye, and went to dinner.

After a good night's rest, an early morning swim, and breakfast, we went back to see Frank. Myrt left me alone with him. He looked much better that day, and we had a long talk.

When I'm with Frank, my senses are alert to his every move, gesture and reaction. I calculate the degrees of our differences and similarities. I can see the reflection of myself in so many ways. As Frank would say with a smile, "It's amazing! God willing, we'll have many years to get to know each other."

Still, when I'm with Frank, there is an uneasiness. Part of it is the guilt and the sense that I have betrayed my Dad, which will persist until I get the courage to tell him. I imagine my state of mind is not unlike that of an adulterer, and wonder if a confession could ever quiet such torment. Could I lose them both? There are times when I accentuate the slightest variance in Frank's attitudes, beliefs or values, as if subconsciously contriving a case to refute that he is my father. That kind of mental trial has effectively removed Rebecca from any endearing relationship as my mother. I don't want to close the door on Frank, as he has become a part of my life.

Frank visited us at our home in January 1987 for a week, meeting my family for the first time. It was a good visit, and he quickly assumed and cultivated his role as grandfather to my sons, spoiling them with his generosity. David visited him in Palm Springs during Berkeley's spring break in April 1987, and they seemed to enjoy each other's company. This was Dave's first opportunity to meet Frank. Later, when I asked David about his visit, he said they played golf, swam and ate lots of homemade spaghetti. Frank commented that Dave's intake was evidence of his Italian heritage. Dave, having been blessed with artistic talents, has always enjoyed drawing portraits, and while he was there, sketched Frank. Dave was amazed at our resemblance, and there was no doubt in his mind that we share the same blood.

During my hospital visit, Frank asked about Rebecca. As I unfolded her story, he winced and let me know he never wanted to see or contact her. She had been an extremely attractive woman in her youth and he was astonished at the description of her grotesque transformation. I brought along some photos of her from the early days, which he recognized right off. I showed a more recent picture, and he couldn't believe it. I mentioned that she had asked about him, to include where he was living, but that I had kept his anonymity. He gave me a stern look and said, "Leave it that way."

I asked him about the incident I had on my home street as a boy, and he denied any knowledge of it. Frank suggested that if anybody had reason and the resources to search for me, it would have been Joan Crawford with her apparent connections through Alice Hough at the Children's Home Society. I hadn't thought of that possibility, but realized if that had been the case, the answer to that mysterious visit was gone forever.

I inquired if he had heard from his son lately. A hurt look was his response. Frank told him about me the past Christmas and things weren't going well between them. He and Joe had been out in his son's garage, when he broke the news. Frank asked, "Joe, what would you think about having an older brother?" His son gave him an incredulous stare as the story of my existence unfolded. Frank said his son's demeanor was a cross between disbelief and anger.

Joe blurted out, "How would you like it if I searched out my real father?"

Frank replied, "That's up to you—be my guest."

When Frank revealed the way he approached his son with this hard information, it seemed to me his manner of delivery had the sensitivity of a sledge hammer. I told Frank I didn't want to come between them; that I somehow felt responsible. He told me not to worry about it, since it wasn't my problem, and that this had been brewing a long time. I could understand the emotional interplay that was involved, and I felt sorry for them. Frank hasn't mentioned if he has told his daughter.

In the fall of 1987, I finally made it to Beaufort, South Carolina for a visit with my brother, Andy Kullberg, and his lovely wife Angela. This was the place where it all began with the first propitious phone call late in April, 1986, and somehow it was fitting that it be my last stop. South Carolina is a beautiful state, and near the coast it has a bayou appearance. I had never been there before. The lush green, thick foliage and enormous trees with Spanish moss dangling from their limbs, were a feast to my eyes. The laid–back lifestyle was perfect for a relaxing visit. Andy has a beautiful Southern Colonial style home, which he and Angela had built. The setting was perfect for our long-awaited reunion.

The evening I arrived, we had champagne, caviar and a gourmet dinner, prepared by Angela. Conversation went on into the night, catching up on the events of the past forty-four years. One night, during my stay, Angela tried her best to teach me Spanish dances, and I ended up playing the castanets with arms arched overhead, and much foot-stomping, until two o'clock that morning. While perusing through photo albums, Andy triggered a reflection from my past. In one of the photos, there was a picture of a nun, and he casually mentioned that when he and ReeAnn were young kids, they referred to nuns as penguins, because of the resemblance to their black and white habits. My parents fondly tell a story about one of my earliest communications when I saw a Catholic nun at about age two. We were walking down a street in my hometown, when a nun approached us and I reportedly said, "Look mommy, a penguin." My parents were both amused and amazed, since they didn't know I realized what a penguin was. Evidently ReeAnn and Andy had taught me.

One afternoon I had the pleasure of meeting my half-sister, Hallie Marie, who was born one week after I left the Kullberg home for the last time. Toward the end of my visit, Andy and I went to a supermarket on an errand, and we ran into a close, long-time friend of Andy's. I saw he was instantly confronted with how to introduce me, and he said, "I'd like you to know my brother, Gary." Later in the car, he said he'd have alot of explaining to do.

George Bauler, my youngest brother, and his family, had dinner with us one Sunday. It was my first opportunity to meet his four young children, who all greeted me as "Uncle Gary" with only occasional coaxing from their parents. While the kids kept busy with games from closet storage, Sue and I had an interesting visit with George and his wife, Brooke, who is a Registered Nurse in Houston. He has been attending an Osteopathic School in Fort Worth, while Brooke and children have remained in Houston, alternating visit locations each weekend.

George lives in an apartment, which he shares. The evening before the Bauler family visit, I called there to confirm times. His roommate answered, saying George was out and would be back in several hours. When I gave my name and message, he said, "Oh yes, I've heard about you. George's mother (Rebecca) called a few minutes ago with an urgent plea for him to call her the minute he gets here—it had something to do with you." I thought, oh hell, what's she up to now? I had never talked with or met George's roommate before, but I had an uneasy feeling he knew more about me than I wished. He told me he'd pass along my message and I thanked him.

After a drink or two, George said with a smile, "Rebecca called yesterday to warn me about you! She said a 'voice' told her that you were going to invite us to your home and strongly urged I decline. She thinks you are an agent or assasin from the Sicilian Mafia, sent by Frank Mazzola!" I laughed and glanced toward Brooke, who looked a little troubled.

She asked, "How could Rebecca have known that you were having us over?"

I smiled and said, "Brooke, don't worry, I'll make it fast and painless!" By the frightened look on her face, it was obvious she didn't appreciate my humor.

I explained, "A week ago, I had called Rebecca to wish her happy birthday, and during our conversation, mentioned that I wanted to have you folks over for dinner." I continued, "And she suggested I invite George when you and the kids were here, so that I could meet your beautiful children. You see, the 'voice' Rebecca heard was mine!" Brooke looked somewhat relieved, but I sensed there still was some suspicion about my true identity. She has known Rebecca for ten years and evidently respects her psychic powers. I never realized my Sicilian features had such a menacing effect on people! Later in the evening, we were in the pool room and I saw Brooke staring at several gallon jugs of Mazzola wine sitting on my bar. She gave me a quizzical look, as if to say, "maybe you are who you say you are, then again, maybe you're not!"

Later, George told me Rebecca is hanging onto the Elvis Presley dream with all her might. She asked him to contact Elvis Presley's brother, who lives in Houston, to see if there was any chance of finding a tidbit she could expand into proof of motherhood. George said, as a boy, he can remember being dragged to Elvis concerts, memorial services and memorabilia shows. Anything having to do with Elvis Presley, they attended, if remotely possible. There were times they hitchhiked across the country to attend Elvis Presley "happenings." He said he'd be surprised if she ever gave it up, and totally accepted me. Her fantasy is so great . . . that she'd always want Elvis to be her son until the day she dies. When I heard that, it bothered me. To be rejected is hard to take. But I understand Rebecca's needs. As she likes to say, "The truth will come in the next life." She knows it now, but will never admit it. Maybe it's just as well, and a blessing in disguise. She has the same tenacity I do, and might force herself into my world, and I'm not sure I want that. Besides, I promised myself not to force my existence on, or cause others anguish for my sake. So be it!

Obsession

My quandary of whether to confess to Dad my discoveries from the "other side" became an all consuming obsession. The same questions would lash out at me over and over, and then again. Would he be able to cope with the realities of what his son had done? The telling would be the easy part. Dad would find my story intriguing and would thoroughly enjoy hearing it. He would tell others about it and enjoy their fascination, as I have. But . . . the time of reckoning would come. In a week, a month—would he still love me? Would he want to share me with those whose blood flows through my veins and whose genetics shaped me? Jealousy is an emotion hard to corral. He was the one who was there when I needed him all my life. Is deceit the answer? He might find out from someone else, and that would be worse yet. If I told him, maybe he would understand. After all, he gave me the box that contained the keys to my past.

What if he became ill on the heels of my disclosure, and God took him from me? My soul ached at the thought of such a possibility. Would he cast me from his heart and mind, disinheriting me of his love, and curse the day I took his name? I asked several friends who had adopted children for their feelings and opinions. Just as I had expected, the responses were mixed and it was clear that there wasn't going to be a simple solution to my dilemma. Several commented, "Why take the chance? Some things are best left unsaid." Others insisted truth was the only route.

Not long ago a friend, who I work with, and his wife adopted a beautiful newborn baby girl. The day of the office baby shower, I went over to congratulate him and we began talking. When I mentioned that I was adopted, he seemed surprised and an affinity grew between us, which often happens with those having similar, personal bonds. He told me that they had waited nearly three years for this happy time to come, and I said that sounded familiar, as my parents had endured about the same waiting period. Their adoption agency went through comparable preliminary applicant screenings, reference checks and home visits.

As I was leaving, I casually mentioned my project and asked if he and his wife would do me the favor of reading an abbreviated version and give their thoughts and opinions. He said they would be happy to, and I delivered a copy to him later in the morning. I didn't give any hint to its content, except to say I'd made an interesting discovery about myself just over a year ago.

Later in the day, I edged my way into the packed reception area, where the baby shower was in progress. What a splendid sight it was! My friend and his wife had a radiant glow about them as they unwrapped each package from the colorful array of gifts for their new baby. I scanned the overcrowded room for the reason of all this cheer and joy, and there she was, the epitome of innocence and preciousness. I simply couldn't take my eyes off her, as she was gently passed among her admirers. I'm not one to frequent such events, but there was something special about that baby shower, which made the affair one I'll never forget. Whether it was because this newborn child was just beginning life's journey, not unlike my own, or that I was fantasizing what my baby shower might have been like, I'm not sure. Its magical spell stayed with me long after I had left.

As I was driving home after work that day, the harsh reality of what I had inadvertently done, suddenly hit me. Probably the last thing my friend and his wife would want to read at this joyous time, was my story of search and discovery. How could I be so insensitive? For what has been elation to me, might well be a nightmare to them. I decided to see him first thing in the morning and apologize. When I went to his office, he was tied up, and I left a message that I had been by. Later he stuck his head in, saying he had read only the first ten pages, but his wife had just called and was fascinated with my story.

The next day he brought the manuscript back, with a sober look about him. The first thing he asked, "Have you told him yet?"

I replied, "No, I'm still not sure how my Dad will take it."

He said, "I hope my daughter will feel she can tell me if she ever decided to. . . to find her natural parents." Almost in the same breath, he said, "But it would hurt to share her with another who wasn't there all her life, and then suddenly wanted to be part of her life. Gary, I hope I never have to face a situation like you have with your dad."

His words came to the heart of the matter and stung a little. How much easier it would have been for him, and comforting too, if I could have said, "I never felt the need to search out my natural parents." I must say the weight of my dilemma is becoming heavy on my soul. God help me!

Susan suggested that I contact and arrange a visit with an old acquaintance of hers, who was associated with a well-known adoption agency in the Dallas-Fort Worth area. I had been looking for more information on current adoption trends, after hearing about my friend's adoption experience. I called one evening, and said if she had the time, I'd be interested to hear her view on the direction the institution of adoption is taking. I told her I was in the middle of writing my life's story, and that I was adopted. She seemed eager to assist, but was curious about my autobiography. I took her a copy, agreeing to get together in a day or two. She called several nights later and admitted that my story had taken her by surprise. She had never heard or read anything quite like it in all her years. She said, "I have time now if you want to come over and talk."

After a few comments about my manuscript, she looked at me and said, "Gary, I'm afraid that closed traditional adoptions are fast becoming a thing of the past. State agencies could eventually give way to private adoption arrange-

211

ments." The demand and supply of "white babies" have dramatically changed over the past twenty years. In the 1960's, couples seeking to adopt white babies had only to be approved, as the supply was plentiful. Birth mothers were relieved just to find an institution that would care for them and their newborns, and hoped parents could be found for their baby's placement. In 1973 that all changed. The Supreme Court of the United States made abortion-on-demand our nationwide policy, when its decision on *Roe vs Wade* was handed down. Since the decision, over twenty million unborn children have been legally aborted. The supply of babies for adoption is such that for every lucky couple, twenty go childless. With babies at a premium, birth mothers have become very demanding. State adoption agencies have been forced to follow the lead of private organizations, which cater almost completely to the birth mother's wishes. The "Openness" philosophy, which gives the natural mother limited access to the child she's giving up, has become a big price to pay by adoption parents. Open communication and contact would seem to dull the role and sanctity of adoption parents, and in the long run, be detrimental to the child.

We started talking about my Dad and whether I should tell him of my discoveries. Susan's friend understood my quandary, and felt only I could make the decision since I knew him best. She debated with herself much as I have done, going back and forth between the viewpoints, and concluded she would lean toward telling him. She has an adopted son who is coming of age, and confessed if he searched and found his natural parents, it would hurt her, but said she'd understand and that time would heal. She admitted her situation was different as she has two daughters of her own, and I'm an only child. Also, my dad is in the omega of his life at eighty-six.

Then she asked, "One thing I'm curious about, do you know if your parents ever had you put in psychological therapy when you were very young?"

I said, "No, not that I'm aware of. Why?"

"Well, when we've had children like you, who experience high stress and abuse as you, it has been necessary to seek professional help for them."

I queried, "Even at such a young age, eighteen months?"

"Yes, even then, the child is very impressionable and can have psychological problems the rest of his life."

That's all I needed to hear! I told her my records never mentioned such counseling, but did indicate my disposition was something less than positive and would take time for me to adjust. That brought to mind one of my conversations with Rebecca. I had given her a small copy of my earliest photos (twenty-two months), since she claimed to have lost any and all photos of me as a baby. Later she remarked, "Gary, your physical appearance looks like my child, but your smiling, happy look in the photo would make me think you can't be mine! The son I lost was very unhappy and miserable; I don't think I ever saw him smile in the last couple months he was with me."

What a damning confession that was! All this reminded me of what the social worker at the Children's Home had said, "You don't want to hear about this, your life was a real mess."

As I was leaving, she pointed to a spot in the middle of her living room floor and said, "That's where I started to read your manuscript and as the pages flew and my excitement grew, I had to tell my husband your extraordinary story. I hope you don't mind." I assured her I didn't, and thanked her for her insights.

I visited Dad for a few days in August, 1987. God, how I wanted to tell him what I had done. To put my arms around him and let the truth flow from my lips. When I was with him, the words wouldn't come. He trusts me and loves me too much. I am his only family left, except for my stepmother's family, who look after him and give him love.

Each year when I visit home, the tongues get sharper as the highballs go down. In my Dad's golden years, verbal archery has been great sport, and arrows fly. Must be nature's way of keeping the mental circuits vibrant. Somehow the atmosphere was just not good for telling him.

My worst nightmare is of Rebecca finding Dad and talking to him. She told me, "I am sent by God to warn people not to let the devil's agents take their children away. They should not let their seed go through fire and damnation to the Evil One. A horrible, horrible sin. People who covet or want other people's children are themselves evil. If they were godly, they would be able to have their own children!" Her confused sense of values are the complete antithesis of Dad's. I cringe, imagining such a confrontation.

After much agonizing and soul-searching, I finally realized I had to tell my Dad. For months I rambled back and forth, always fearing that to confess my act of discovery, would make me a Judas in his eyes. It wasn't until Susan hinted that my well–being could be at stake, that I came to my senses. I was becoming a nervous wreck. It was so bad that every time I talked with Dad on the phone, or received a letter from him, I would cringe with fear until it was clear that he hadn't found out my secret. God, I didn't need that hanging over me until the day he died. Even then, I imagined I would somehow feel guilt for not telling him. I had no choice, I had to tell him. It came down to a question of when.

A good friend sent a note after reading my story, which helped me come to a decision. She wrote, "Give yourself permission to love your dad and Frank, and don't feel guilty about it. God let you find Frank and your past, just as He let your mom and dad find you. Enjoy all of them in this life while they are still here."

In January 1988, I planned a March trip to visit Dad. When and how would I tell him? It had to be when there was just the two of us. I considered confiding with several hometown friends first, to get their reaction as to how Dad would receive my story. But I knew I was only deceiving myself, and looking for a way out. If anybody knew Dad, I was the one. There was no substitute. But, in truth, I didn't know how he'd take it. Ultimately, the responsibility rested with me, and Dad should be the first to hear my story.

214

As February came to a close, my anxiety level was running high. The flight to Los Angeles International was set, along with the rental car arrangements. I had called Dad and told him I would arrive in the evening of March 3, 1988. He was looking forward to my visit. I was staying three days, but planned to tell him at the earliest opportunity, so he'd have a chance to sort things out, and become as comfortable as possible with this revelation before I returned home. It had taken me months to assimilate these new and strange discoveries of my life, and it would take time for Dad, as well.

After boarding on American Airlines, I felt confined and uneasy with the task before me. It was an early afternoon flight, and normally I don't imbibe then, but this time I had the stewardess bring me several double Scotches during the three hour flight. At one point, I remember asking God to please give my Dad understanding and comfort when I told him my story. I had decided that tomorrow I'd suggest going for coffee at one of the resort hotels along the harbor. My flight arrived on time at LAX. By the time I picked up my rental car, I had walked off nervous energy and the effect of the Scotches. For a Thursday, LAX seemed unusually packed with cars, taxis, busses and people rushing to catch flights. Ninety minutes later, I pulled into my dad's driveway.

As always, he seemed to be in good spirits and health. I put my things away and we visited. Our schedule for the coming day was going to be busy. Dad had several errands and social calls planned for the morning. Early in the afternoon my step-sister was flying in from Vermont. Finding time to tell him my story was going to be difficult.

The next morning we took our usual early walk. We didn't see many of his friends and the walk went fast. I casually mentioned there was something I needed to discuss with him, and suggested we go for coffee later in the morning at one of the harbor hotels. He nodded and let it pass . . . Dad probably thought I was going to hit him up for a loan, as had happened on several past "serious" occasions.

215

By late morning, we had completed our scheduled stops. I headed for the harbor area and time was running short. During the ride, Dad was quiet. He was waiting for me to break the subject. I could feel my heart quicken and a thin layer of sweat form over my body. The time for cleansing the soul was at hand. I glanced over at Dad as I drove. What I was about to tell him could change his life just as it had mine. . . for a moment, I was ready to put off telling him.

Then, as if I was outside my body, I heard myself say, "Dad, I have something I must tell you . . . first, above all else, I want you to know how much I love you. . . remember that box of baby records you gave me . . . almost two years ago I made contact . . ."

We never made it for coffee that morning. Dad gestured toward a beachside parking area, and I pulled in. We found a path that meandered along the beach, and followed it to a bench. All the time I continued the telling. The flow of my words seemed to follow the relentless cadence of the sea. Dad was still and his sunglasses kept me from seeing his eyes. A man came by, walking his dog, and Dad reached out to pet him. The stranger paused as Dad lovingly stroked his four-legged friend. That was when I knew Dad was going to be alright . . . for now.

Epilogue

Any deep-seated hangup I had about being adopted has left me. I'm proud of being adopted and would shout it from the rooftops. I'm free! I know who I am.

Life can twist and turn, ebb and flow in so many mysterious ways. I had always thought of my life as being somewhat unremarkable. Little did I know! I never considered myself to be a very lucky person. I must have used up my share of good luck, and then some, during the first eighteen months of my life when I found Dad and Mom.

I've told my story many times to immediate family and close friends. It gives me pleasure to share it and observe their emotional reactions. After the telling, I'd often get a penetrating stare into my eyes, as if my friends were trying to look directly into my soul. They wanted to know if my journey into the past had changed me. Had I seen the "Oz" of my past? Was I a different person? Occasionally, they'd ask with concern, "How can you accommodate the dichotomy of backgrounds, parents, families and values?" They'd ask, "How did you keep from blowing your mind?" Some took the soothing and reassuring approach. Something like, "This won't change you, you're the same old Gary."

I must confess my odyssey was a super "mind ride", and at times, I lost contact with reality. Sometimes I'd catch myself daydreaming about what might have been—the many lives I might have lived. It was a miracle that I was

217

born into this life, and that I made it through the ordeal in the Berkeley Avenue house. All these things had an emotional impact on me, and I'm sure I've changed a little.

As I ponder over my trip and all the roads I have traveled through my life's universe, in the end, it isn't unlike waking from a dream. Two years have passed since I dared to enter through the portal to my mysterious past—to the "other side". I have gone back and forth through that time warp at risk of upending my rational being. In defense, my mind has tended to short–circuit automatically, returning to the more familiar and comfortable existence I have known. Even now, after all this time, I have often had to remind myself that I have discovered my past—that the "other side" of my life is now part of my life. The reality of it still startles and amazes me.

I have no regrets. If there was one, I would have enjoyed meeting Joan Crawford again as an adult. That would have been a story unto itself. I shouldn't be greedy. I am fulfilled. My cup runneth over! Everyone should write his story. It's wonderfully therapeutic. Even though I know Dad is sensitive about my occasional contact with the "Other Side," he has never openly protested and has respected my decision to continue those relationships . . . and I love him that much more for it.